Robert Howie

Reply to Letter of Professor Blaikie, D.D., LL.D., to Rev. Andrew A. Bonar, D.D.

On Statement Issued on the Dods and Bruce Cases

Robert Howie

Reply to Letter of Professor Blaikie, D.D., LL.D., to Rev. Andrew A. Bonar, D.D.
On Statement Issued on the Dods and Bruce Cases

ISBN/EAN: 9783337066703

Printed in Europe, USA, Canada, Australia, Japan

Cover: Foto ©ninafisch / pixelio.de

More available books at **www.hansebooks.com**

REPLY TO LETTER

OF

PROFESSOR BLAIKIE, D.D., LL.D.,

TO

REV. ANDREW A. BONAR, D.D.,

ON STATEMENT ISSUED

ON THE DODS AND BRUCE CASES.

BY

REV. ROBERT HOWIE, M.A.

*SECOND EDITION WITH POSTSCRIPT,
COMPLETING FIVE THOUSAND.*

GLASGOW:
DAVID BRYCE AND SON.
EDINBURGH: ANDREW ELLIOT.
1890.

PRICE SIXPENCE.

REPLY.

THE following letters to Dr. Blaikie on the Dods and Bruce cases (Appendix I.) were sent to him in reply to letters received from him immediately after the rising of last Assembly. As his letters to me related to a public question, and to my action in public, and as he had written to me twelve years before on the same subject (in connection with the former case against Dr. Dods, while two years afterwards he again opened communications regarding it), I intimated to him that, on this occasion, *I reserved my right to publish* my replies, and at the same time requested permission to publish his letters to me. That permission he refused, on the ground that his letters to me were "private," and that if they had been intended for publication they would have been written in a different form. At the same time, he intimated that he was anxiously considering the duty of bringing some views on the subject before the public. So long as he advocated his views in private, I did not feel at liberty to drag them to light, notwithstanding the special reservation of my right to publish my side of the correspondence. Now, however, that he has in his Letter to Dr. Bonar, just published, animadverted on the "Statement" for which, equally with Dr. Bonar and others, I am responsible, and has, at the same time, given expression, though in a somewhat more expanded form, to the views previously communicated to me, I feel that I do him no injustice when I now publish my letters. I do this the rather because it will be seen that, *by anticipation*, I have in these letters replied to the leading statements in regard to Holy Scripture made in the published Letter to Dr. Bonar.

Though I regret to differ from Dr. Blaikie, for whom I have a high personal regard, I am not sorry that, by the publication of his Letter to Dr. Bonar, he has thrown new light upon the real meaning and import of the deliverance of last Assembly, in the case of Dr. Dods, as also by implication in the case of Dr. Bruce, though, strange to say, he has not a word about the latter—except on the Title-page.

This complete silence on the part of Dr. Blaikie in regard to the latter case, as also in regard to the views of Dr. Dods on the Divinity, Atonement, and Resurrection of our Lord, is very noteworthy, the more especially when account is taken of the large amount of space occupied by references to these matters in the "Statement" so severely criticized. How is his complete silence on these points to be explained? Is it because Dr. Blaikie felt that, even with his own loose views on Inspiration, and his eagerness to vindicate his colleague to the utmost, he could not conscientiously say a single word in the way of defending or even apologizing for the statements made by Dr. Dods in regard to the Divinity, Atonement, and Resurrection of our Lord, and that he could far less justify, even to the smallest extent, the utterances of Dr. Bruce referred to in the "Statement"? If these were the reasons for the ominous silence of Dr. Blaikie on these points, surely as he seeks to explain his vote in the case of Dr. Dods (with what amount of success I leave the readers of his Letter to judge) it was still more imperative on him to try also to explain his vote in the case of Dr. Bruce, in favour of a motion which not only declares that there is "no ground for a process against him as teaching doctrine opposed to the Standards of the Church," but "represents feebly and inadequately the gravity of the case," and even "fails to give adequate expression to the strongly condemnatory opinion of the College Sub-Committee."

But whatever his reasons for so complete a silence in the case of Dr. Bruce, the interpretation he gives of the meaning of the deliverance in the case of Dr. Dods, and the explanation he gives of his own vote, show very clearly the justice of the severe strictures passed on that deliverance by those who compiled the "Statement." I know that an earnest attempt has been made since last Assembly to quiet the fears and anxieties of those who were alarmed by the continual reiteration, by Dr. Dods, of the view that there were "errors" in the Scriptures as originally given, and of the view that some of the things "commended, or even commanded" in the Old Testament were "immoralities." They have been given to understand that the deliverance of the Assembly contained an emphatic condemnation of the views in question, and that no minister or professor of the Church would dare, after such a condemnation, to propagate these views anew in public. In proof of these averments, their attention has been called to the terms of the deliverance, viz.: "She (the Church) views the use of the term 'mistakes and immoralities' to describe recognized difficulties in the Scriptures as utterly unwarranted, and fitted to give grave offence." They have been assured, moreover, that the opening words of the deliverance (viz., that "The writings of Dr. Dods do not afford ground for instituting a process against him as teaching what is at variance with the Standards of the Church") do not grant ecclesiastical toleration to his views in regard to Holy Scripture, but simply mean that, in the judgment of the Assembly, it was not advisable or expedient to institute a process.

If the anxieties of any have been really allayed by such a mode of interpreting the deliverance of the Assembly, the published Letter of Dr. Blaikie will doubtless come to them as a strange surprise. It will show them what is the real meaning to be attached to that deliverance. It will give them, moreover, most convincing proof that the very views in regard to Holy Scripture, supposed by them to be condemned and not tolerated, are now publicly re-affirmed and even defended at great length. These views have been so re-affirmed by Dr. Dods in an article in the *British Weekly*, of date October 2, 1890. That article (which so flagrantly misrepresents the opinions of those opposed to him, whom he describes as "uninstructed Evangelicals," who "have been combining with Secularists, Atheists, and anti-Christians in general, to betray the Christian position") is only what, in view of his previous misrepresentations and "intemperate" utterances, might have been expected of Dr. Dods, and proves conclusively that he at least does not intend to be silenced in regard to his favourite tenets by the deliverance of last Assembly. The attitude now publicly assumed by Dr. Blaikie will probably be of still greater use in opening the eyes of the public to the real meaning and import of that deliverance. When it is seen that he publicly adopts, and even argues in defence of the views supposed to be condemned by the Assembly, and justifies his joining in that *apparent* condemnation, on the ground that it referred not to the views themselves, but simply to the "*form and manner*" in which they were expressed by Dr. Dods; when, moreover, he complains that even in this qualified condemnation there was exhibited, on the part of the Assembly, a tendency to "*hysterics*," it will doubtless be generally felt that a deliverance so skilfully constructed as to enable its supporters thus "to hunt with the hounds and run with the hare" cannot carry much weight, either as a condemnation of error, or as a vindication of Divine truth. I am curious to know whether Drs. Adam and Rainy endorse the interpretation now publicly given by Dr. Blaikie of the meaning of the deliverance of the Assembly.

In his Letter to Dr. Bonar, Dr. Blaikie stigmatizes as a "most uncharitable document," the "Statement" on which he animadverts. He rebukes us for being "so combative," "when we might be conciliatory." He is "amazed" because those who subscribe the "Statement" venture, in a perfectly respectful manner, to intimate to their brethren that "grave questions will arise as to the possibility of a Church whose members are not at one on matters so fundamental continuing united," if, after the use of all competent means, "an equally authoritative declaration" cannot be obtained from a future Assembly, such as will rectify the wrong done by last Assembly, and make it manifest that the Church still believes (even as she asks her ministers and professors to declare, before ordination or induction, that they believe) "the Scriptures of the Old and New Testament to be the Word of God;" that "God (who is Truth itself)" is the "Author thereof"; and that, as given by their Divine Author, they are of "infallible truth and Divine authority."

Without fear of contradiction, I venture to say that Dr.

Blaikie is the last man in the Church who should express himself in the way I have just indicated. In his first letter to me, of date April 20, 1878—a letter to which no mark of privacy was attached—he informed me that if the views were "enforced" which I then publicly advocated in regard to Holy Scripture, and which were the same as those I now advocate, he "should have to leave the Church, or at least resign" his "professorship." Moreover at last Assembly we were told that our request could not be granted, when some of us urged the leaders to omit the opening statement from the motion of Dr. Adam, and when we assured them that if that were done, we could see our way to vote for it, believing, as we did, that in the body of the motion there was a *bonâ fide* condemnation of the *views* of Dr. Dods in regard to Holy Scripture, and not merely of the "*form of expression.*" We could have done this, without doing violence to our consciences, though we did not regard it, even when thus amended, as entirely satisfactory. The main reason given for the refusal of our request was that some of those consulted in the framing of the motion, and who were expected to support it, would on no account agree to such an omission of what was considered by them its most essential part. In this connection the name of Dr. Blaikie transpired. We were told that if the opening words were omitted, some 300 ministers might leave the Church, or might require to be taken under discipline. In view of these facts, it ill becomes Dr. Blaikie to rebuke his brethren for the want of a "conciliatory" spirit, and for hinting "ominously at a coming disruption."

Those who have issued the "Statement" do not wish "disruption," far less do their words imply secession. For myself I would deplore even "disruption" as one of the greatest of calamities, and will do all I conscientiously can to prevent it.

In point of fact, as I have the means of knowing, the issuing of our "Statement," so far from tending to bring about a "disruption," has meanwhile prevented many persons from at once leaving the Church in consequence of the decisions of last Assembly, affording as it does a means of publicly protesting against these decisions, and thus, so far, giving present relief to aggrieved consciences. As showing, on the one hand, the strength of conviction held on this subject, and on the other, that the "Statement" is not extreme, it is noteworthy that almost the only objections taken to it have been that our strictures on the decisions of the Assembly are not severe enough, and that the action we propose is not sufficiently energetic. Not a few are displeased, and some have even withheld their adherence to the "Statement," because in it we do not commit ourselves to an immediate "agitation" through public meetings, but rather propose that "in the first instance" an opportunity should be given to the radical courts of the Church of saying whether they are prepared to overture next General Assembly to rectify the wrong done by last Assembly—in so far as it can be rectified—by giving, apart from the views of individuals, a clear and unambiguous declaration of the belief of the Church in regard to Holy Scripture—a declaration in harmony (1) with the doctrine hitherto maintained by the Church, (2) with the plain import of the Confession of Faith, (3) with the testimony of Scripture regarding itself, and (4) with the testimony of our Lord Himself.

But while those who compiled the "Statement" have thus done their best to prevent the separation of individuals from the Church, and even "agitation" through public meetings, until it is seen whether the Church Courts are prepared to take any action in the matter, it is just as well that our brethren should know, that there are certain truths so vital and fundamental—so connected with the honour of God—so intertwined with all our personal hopes of salvation, and the maintenance of which is so essential to the true prosperity of the Church and the success of the Gospel ministry—that many of us could not, with a good conscience, continue permanently in connection with a Church which, after her testimony in regard to them has been tarnished, would persistently refuse to give, when asked to do so, a clear and unambiguous declaration of her belief in regard to them.

And the truths which Dr. Blaikie seems to controvert in his Letter to Dr. Bonar are of that nature.

Dr. Blaikie represents the issuing of the "Statement" as a "new agitation," which Dr. Bonar and others "propose to institute," and declares that it "will keep up noise, discontent, and strife, without succeeding in its aim."

The agitation is not "new," and the responsibility for it and for the "noise, discontent, and strife," with which it has been, or may yet be accompanied, must be placed on the right shoulders. Dr. Blaikie himself wrote thus to an American paper at the beginning of this year:—"There is a strong feeling against him (*i.e.*, Dr. Dods), too, for having caused so much pain to good men, and so much disturbance to the Church without any attempt to mitigate the distress he occasioned." And yet Dr. Blaikie now joins him in causing pain to good men, and seeks to blame them for the "disturbance" it may occasion.

In the days of Israel's degeneracy, Ahab put the question, "Art thou he that troubleth Israel?" He was quickly silenced by the cutting response of the fearless prophet of Jehovah:—"I have not troubled Israel; but thou, and thy father's house, in that ye have forsaken the commandments of the Lord, and thou hast followed Baalim."

Commenting on these words, and referring specially to the state of things in Germany, where the views so strenuously defended by Dr. Blaikie had their origin and in which their full effect has become manifest, Krummacher writes as follows: —"What is the sin which Elijah expressly holds up to him as the proper source of the whole calamity? Is it his intemperance, his covetousness, his frivolity, his unchaste life? No, it is his shameless unbelief; it is his wanton departure from God's Word and statutes; it is his blasphemous contempt of what the living God had revealed and appointed in the world. Blessed God, if this be the deepest crime, and the blackest guilt in God's sight; if, for this cause, He visits nations and countries and cities with fire and sword; what have we to look for in an age wherein the forsaking of God's statutes is become the fashion, and a heathenish rationalism has found its way into the very cottage and the workshop; when the language of the wicked servant, 'we will not have this man to reign over us,' is becoming always more general, and the sound of error is heard from so many pulpits and seats of learning, from the highest to the lowest, as a real voice of Baal; in which true Christianity, the belief of the forgiveness of sins through the blood of the Lamb, is so frequently branded as *mysticism;* and the real life of the soul in the Holy Ghost, the life of love to the Saviour, and walking in His footsteps, is so often decried as *fanaticism;* and when Baal has so many worshippers, who, in the gloom of Pantheism or Atheism, scatter their incense in his nostrils, and build him altars? How will it at length fare with such a generation, if we do not in good time fall weeping before the uplifted rod in the hand of the great Preserver of men?"

Very likely Dr. Blaikie may be ready to reply that this state of things in Germany is only one of the illustrations of how "it is quite possible that any concession on inspiration would be taken advantage of by some for illegitimate purposes." In view of his contention on this point, it is surely a somewhat suggestive and startling coincidence, that in the very number of the *British Weekly* (that, viz., of Oct. 30), which contains a highly laudatory notice of the Letter of Dr. Blaikie to Dr. Bonar, there is placed alongside of it the following statement, which shows that in Holland "concessions on inspiration" have produced the same kind of fruit as in Germany:—" The goal of 'the followers of the more advanced school of New Testament studies' in Holland has surely been reached. We are informed by the *Scottish Review* that a new handbook of religious instruction has been published there, the writer of which thus summarizes for Dutch children the facts underlying the Gospel: 'All that can be said to be historically certain is that there lived among the Jews of the past days, a commanding religious personality, to the partial narrative of whose life various spirits felt themselves drawn to contribute.' Here is a power unto salvation! Some among ourselves are looking with hope to something remarkably like it."

When such admissions as to the practical outcome in Holland of "concessions on inspiration" find their way even into the columns of the *British Weekly*, Drs. Dods, Bruce, and Blaikie ought to beware lest similar advantage be taken by-and-bye in Scotland, of the concessions they make or endorse, and thus that they be held responsible before God and man for like disastrous results of their teaching.

After his striking article on "The Old Pulpit and the New" (in *The Theological Review* of April last), I am "amazed" that Dr. Blaikie should stigmatize, as "an argument of unbelief," all that appears in the "Statement" under the third heading, viz., "*Because the view now tolerated alters entirely the relation of the Church and of the individual to the Scriptures, and is sure to lead to their rejection even as a Rule of Faith and Life.*"

It would have been more to the point if he had attempted to meet the argument as it is there put. But that apart, in the article to which I have referred, Dr. Blaikie more than justifies the anxiety felt by many of his brethren as to the possible developments of "the new critical views." He admits that grave changes in the preaching of our younger ministers have already taken place. He begins his article by telling how he had, at the close of the preceding session, protested against a charge made by a correspondent of *The Nonconformist*, viz., that "It was notorious that many of the younger ministers of the Free Church had not only adopted the new critical views, but had entirely given up the old evangelical lines, and were preaching in a strain not a whit higher than that of the late Dean Stanley." Six months after he had thus uttered his protest, he is constrained to say :—" I am not sure that I should have written so decidedly to-day as I did then." "There *is* a change," he adds, "in the preaching of many of the younger ministers of the Free Church, though it is far from amounting to what has been alleged." Thereafter he goes on to describe "the change" in words that form a severe accusation against the younger ministers of a Church, that has hitherto been specially distinguished for its fearless proclamation of evangelical doctrine. "It is not," he says, "like a return to the cold and heartless moderatism of last century. It is often the preaching of earnest men bent on raising the spiritual and moral life of their people. The complaint that I hear against it is that there is not much of Christ in it; or, if He be set forth, it is His Person and personal influence that are dwelt on; but there is not much of His Atonement, nor of the plan of Salvation for lost sinners. It does not deal with men as children of wrath who have to be saved from condemnation. It does not make evident the difference between the converted and unconverted, and seldom appeals to men on the ground that 'they must be born again.' It would rather improve men and raise them up heavenward than regenerate them . . . With reference to this style of preaching, the complaint that older hearers make is that while Christ is presented very fully as an example and as an influence, He is not brought prominently forward as an atoning Saviour. It is also complained that often, in historical and expository lectures, amid much that is most interesting, there is little or no mention of Christ at all."

This style of preaching Dr. Blaikie powerfully contrasts with that of Disruption times, and utters such seasonable and wholesome warnings as to the disastrous results that may be expected to follow, that for the service thus rendered he deserves the cordial thanks of all who love the old Gospel and the truth as it is in Jesus.

But when Dr. Blaikie thus wrote as to these new-born tendencies in the Free Church pulpit, I wonder that it never occurred to him that such preaching as he deprecates is but the *natural outcome* of the views in regard to Holy Scripture he now advocates in his Letter to Dr. Bonar. At all events, seeing he has felt it to be his duty to sound the note of alarm in connection with "the new" pulpit, I humbly submit that he need not be quite so irate when his brethren utter their solemn, united, public protest against the new views of inspiration, which in other lands have not only led to "the entire subversion both of the objective truth and the binding authority of the Bible," but to the repudiation of evangelical doctrine, and even to the denial of the Supernatural. (See Appendix II.)

He tells us that we should desist, because, forsooth, our "agitation will keep up noise, discontent, and strife, without succeeding in its aim."

I have yet to learn that success in obtaining majorities in Church Courts is the standard of duty in bearing testimony to Divine truth. Martyrs, Confessors, and Covenanters did not so reason. Elijah did not so reason when alone he confronted, on the heights of Carmel, the 450 prophets of Baal. Notwithstanding the disparity in numbers, he did the very thing which Dr. Blaikie seems to deprecate. He made an appeal to the people. He sought to rouse their consciences against the prevailing idolatry. Nor was the appeal in vain. Jehovah answered by fire. "And when all the people saw it they fell on their faces: and they said, The Lord He is the God; the Lord He is the God."

The Lord God of Elijah can yet answer by fire, in a still more glorious manner—can baptize with the Holy Ghost and with fire—and can, with such a baptism, give experimental proof, even to "common people," that the Bible is indeed His own Word of "infallible truth and Divine authority." Dr. Blaikie should not be quite so confident, therefore, that failure will attend our testimony among the people, even though, as he predicts, the Church Courts (to whom, in the first instance, we intend to make our appeal) should unhappily decide by majorities in favour of the views he publicly defends,—even though a majority of the ministers of the Free Church of Scotland should declare that they personally hold that there were "errors" in the Scriptures as originally given, and that "immoralities" were "commended, or even commanded," in the Old Testament.

From the oracular manner in which Dr. Blaikie declares that, "carried out to its proper conclusions," our "Statement" "would require a majority of the ministers of our Church to be subjected to discipline," it is plain that he has persuaded himself that all who voted for the motion of Mr. Renny in last Assembly, and a great many more, personally hold the views in regard to Holy Scripture which he publicly defends.

Considering the ability and prominent position of those who propagate these views; the special access they have to the receptive minds of young men now studying for the holy ministry; the apologies made for these views even by ecclesiastical leaders who declare that they personally dislike them; the sanction given them by the declaration of last Assembly as not being "at variance with the Standards of the Church"; the reputation for culture and scholarship a young man obtains through espousing them; the adulation which is sure to be lavished by a certain class of newspapers on the man who thus throws old-fashioned beliefs to the winds; the contempt and scorn poured on those who dare to stand in the old paths, even though it be in fulfilment of solemn ordination vows—considering all these things, I am prepared to admit that the amount of sympathy manifested (especially among the younger ministers of the Church) with the new views of Holy Scripture now advocated by Drs. Dods, Bruce, and Blaikie, is alarming enough.

But after making due allowance for all the untoward and powerful forces at work, I will not believe that a majority of the ministers of the Free Church personally hold that there were "errors" and "immoralities" in the original Scriptures, until I see it demonstrated by a decisive vote on the merits of the question at issue—a vote uninfluenced by the engaging personality of a Professor, and in which the Church will simply declare her own testimony to the "infallible truth and Divine Authority" of the Word of God, in all its statements—its statements of fact, as well as of doctrine and duty.

I am confirmed in the belief that things are not yet quite so bad as they seem, because not a few of those who voted for the motion of Mr. Renny (including even some most prominent in its advocacy), have assured me, since the Assembly, that they personally agree with the views I advocate, and that equally with myself they condemn the views of Dr. Dods. They usually add, that they condemn still more emphatically the views of Dr. Bruce. So many indeed have thus spoken to me, that I still cling to the hope that when, in our Church Courts and in the Confession of Faith Committee, the matter comes up for discussion, it may happily yet be found that among our ministers generally, and even among our Professors, there is, after all, less divergence of view than at present appears.

I cling the rather to this hope, because the published Letter of Dr. Blaikie shows plainly that he occupies an utterly untenable position on this whole question—a position from which I hope he will be driven as the controversy proceeds. He makes certain admissions in regard to the Word of God which are utterly inconsistent with the view for which he so eagerly contends throughout his Letter. It is evident, moreover, that he is labouring under some misconceptions as to the views of those whose "Statement" he criticises. These misconceptions seem to warp his judgment on the question as a whole.

It is true that he has so profited by what I said in my first letter on the point, that at length he has got rid of the delusion that those opposed to Dr. Dods contend for "verbal dictation," or, in other words, for the "theory of mechanical inspiration." He is at last candid enough to admit that the theory in question "is now all but abandoned." As this "theory of mechanical inspiration" is the man of straw at which the batteries of Dr. Dods and his supporters have for years been directed, let us hope that when, on the testimony of Dr. Blaikie, they discover that such a theory is "now all but abandoned," they will forthwith cease from industriously placing a false issue before the Church, by representing us as contending for that theory. I adhere to what I published on this point 12 years ago :—" I know of no one who holds such a theory. For myself, I cannot apply the word 'mechanical' either to the Spirit of God or to the spirit of man. On the contrary, we hold that the sacred writers were not machines in any sense; that their mental powers were not superseded; that there was no interference with the exercise of their distinctive mental peculiarities and idiosyncrasies. Instead of holding the mechanical theory, we will do all we can to prevent the Church from being committed to any theory on the subject. What we deem essential is not the *mode*, but the *product* of inspiration, viz., a Book of 'infallible truth and Divine authority.'"

But while Dr. Blaikie at length admits that "the theory of mechanical inspiration" is "now all but abandoned," he criticises our "Statement," on the supposition that somehow we are seeking to commit the Church to the views of Dr. Cunningham or of Dr. Hodge, or to what has been called "plenary verbal inspiration." Now, while it is doubtless true that many who subscribe the "Statement" do believe in "verbal inspiration," (even as Dr. Blaikie in a letter written to me ten years ago said, in correction of a statement previously made by him,—" I do believe in verbal *inspiration*, what I cannot receive is verbal *dictation*") it is a noteworthy fact that from the beginning to the end of the "Statement," there is not a single word commit-

ting any one who signs it to "*verbal inspiration*," far less any proposal to commit the Church to it. What we contend for is such a doctrine of inspiration as implies immunity from error for all the statements of the Scriptures as originally given. In other words, we accept the phraseology employed by the College Sub-Committee in describing the views of some of its members. We "believe all statements of the original Scriptures to be true in the sense divinely intended: that sense being also consistent with a fair use of words, within the range of legitimate human speech." We are simply amazed that there should be a single member of the College Committee who does not accept *that* as a statement of his personal belief. So little, moreover, do we contend, as Dr. Blaikie supposes we do, for "*ipsissima verba*," in the case of reported speeches, that we go out of our way to express agreement with the College Sub-Committee when it makes the following statement, which I now quote *in extenso* because of its value in this connection:—
"While different views may be taken of the doctrine of Inspiration, all views alike are consistent with admitting different accounts of the same transactions. Accounts may vary in the expression, in the fulness or the compression of the report, in the aspects which receive emphasis or prominence, and yet be *all alike true*, and each valuable in its own kind and from its own point of view. As regards reports of sayings and discourses, inspiration does not guarantee verbatim reporting, more than any other kind of reporting. Discourses may be reproduced (more or less fully) in the very words used, or only in their effect and substance; and there is no reason why inspiration should not avail itself of any or all of the ways in which reliable accounts can be given. It is of some importance for the expositor to judge correctly on what principle the reports he deals with have been framed."

I have italicized the words "all alike true," because they constitute the pivot on which this controversy turns. We affirm that whatever variety there may be in the forms of expression, the accounts are "all alike true," and especially that they are "true in the sense divinely intended; that sense being also consistent with a fair use of words, within the range of legitimate human speech." We hold that there may be *a true summary of a discourse as well as a true verbatim report.* We hold further that there may be a true record of the sayings of men or devils, even though these sayings may themselves be untrue, for they may be truthfully recorded under the guidance of the inspiring Spirit, in order that they may be refuted by counter-statements of Divine truth, or in order that human or Satanic wickedness may be set in a true light.

Dr. Blaikie writes as if we contended that the Bible is the Word of God, *in the sense of containing only the direct utterances of God Himself,* as the immediate speaker for the time being. As, twelve years ago, I approvingly quoted the statement of Dr. Fairbairn bearing on this point, cited in my second letter, and as I then said that " We all hold that there are other things in the Bible beside ' Divine Revelation strictly so-called ; ' " that " it contains a record of human affairs, of the sayings and doings of men and angels, as well as of the sayings and doings of God," I am at a loss to know why Dr. Blaikie should so express himself as to imply that we hold that there is nothing else in the Bible but " God's very words."

I am also at a loss to know why he should seek to make it appear that we deny that there was the use, by inspired writers, of "pre-existing""uninspired writings or statements." Dr. Blaikie asks, "What are we to infer" from the fact of the incorporation of these into the Scriptures? His own reply is, " Simply that the Holy Ghost guaranteed their substantial accuracy and allowed their use, but not that He stood sponsor for every word." Who, I wonder, ever supposed that when " pre-existing Documents " were used, or when " quotations are given from Greek and other pagan poets," the documents so used or the words so quoted were " inspired," or that the Holy Ghost " stood sponsor for every word " ?

When in these pages, of which I am undoubtedly the author, I quote here and there, sentences from the Letter of Dr. Blaikie, do I thereby become " sponsor for every word " I quote, or do I even guarantee " the substantial accuracy " of what is quoted ? No ; I quote some sentences with the view of showing that Dr. Blaikie makes statements, not merely substantially, but totally inaccurate, and I become "sponsor" neither for his words, nor for his ideas, by the mere act of quoting. Everything depends on the use I make of the quotations in my own production, whether in the way of approval or of disapproval. If I make a quotation from his Letter, and express approval of the idea or truth it contains, I become to that extent " sponsor " for that, but even in this case, every one knows that the idea or truth is expressed not in my words, but in the words of Dr. Blaikie. On the other hand, if I express disapproval of the idea or truth contained in the quotation, I become " sponsor " not for it, but for what I say in its refutation. Apply these plain commonsense principles to the Word of God, and there can be no difficulty in seeing that Dr. Fairbairn is right when he says that, " In speaking of the inspiration of Scripture, respect must be had to the distinctive characteristics of its several parts. And where the sentiment uttered, or the circumstances recorded, cannot, from its obvious connection or import, be ascribed to God, the inspiration of the writer is to be viewed as appearing simply in the faithfulness of the record, or the adaptation of the matter contained in it to its place in the sacred volume. Were it but a human idea, or a thought even from the bottomless pit, yet the right setting of the idea, or the just treatment of the thought, may as truly require the guidance of the unerring Spirit, as the report of a message from the upper Sanctuary."

If Dr. Blaikie had kept in view these obvious distinctions, he would not have ventured to cite the admitted use of preexisting materials as his *first argument* in proof of the view that there were " errors " in the Scriptures as originally given. A more grotesque line of argument, than the one followed on that point, I cannot well conceive, betraying as it does from first to last the strangest confusion of ideas.

In order to make out a case of so-called " error " under that head, Dr. Blaikie says that the Holy Ghost " accepted " " Matthew's forty-two generations, or three fourteens (Matt. i. 17), copied doubtless from the national archives, although we know that there are omissions in them, rendering them not absolutely correct." Here he assumes that there was error in the national archives copied by Matthew, and " accepted " or endorsed by the Holy Ghost.

Surely another explanation might be given, viz., that although there was no error whatever in the national archives (and it is not likely that there was), Matthew, for a special purpose, made a selection from them, under the guidance of the Holy Ghost, and that the genealogy as given by him is "true in the sense divinely intended"—the divine intention obviously being not to give all the links in the chain of our Lord's descent from Adam, but simply to give as many as would show, in fulfilment of the Divine promise, His unbroken descent, first from Adam through the line of Seth to Noah; then from Noah through the line of Shem to Abraham; then through the line of Isaac, Jacob, Judah, and David to Christ. With such an end in view, only such details were given as were needed, but all given are "true in the sense divinely intended." Matthew does not profess to give every link, and so far from copying the improbable "error" of the national archives, Alford is doubtless right when, commenting on verse 2, he says that "these additions" (and his brethren) "probably indicate that Matthew did not take his genealogy from any family or public documents, but constructed it himself."

The division in Matthew's table into three fourteens is in perfect accordance with a very common practice among the Jews respecting genealogies. They thus resorted to artificial arrangements for the purpose of assisting the memory. As Dr. Fairbairn says, "Arrangements of this sort would naturally lead to abbreviations of some of the divisions; as here, in the second portion of Matthew's table, three links are left out to restrict the number to fourteen. It is very probable, also, that some were omitted in the last division; since for the fourteen of Matthew, we have twenty-two in Luke. But such omissions were constantly made in the genealogical tables, even when there was no such purpose to be served by it; and was indeed rendered necessary by the inconvenient length to which the tables, when kept in full, often extended." Let the expositor once get hold of the principle on which Matthew, under the guidance of the inspiring Spirit, proceeded in constructing his table, and I defy him to prove that there is any statement whatever made by Matthew "not absolutely correct."

The second argument used by Dr. Blaikie in favour of the view that there were errors in the original Scriptures, that, viz., based on "quotations," is equally inept and inconclusive.

The fact referred to by him in connection with quotations from other parts of Scripture is not disputed. We all admit that "the quotation often differs from the original." But the question here is not as to the fact, but as to the proper explanation of the fact, and the inference to be drawn from it. Such a practice is no proof whatever that there were "errors" in the Scriptures as originally given, and one is surprised that Dr. Blaikie should seek to use it for such a purpose. When it is remembered that the Bible, although written by different human authors, had one Divine Author throughout, any difficulty which the fact occasions immediately disappears. Just as Dr. Blaikie himself may, in other of his writings, (in a different connection, in a somewhat modified form, and for a slightly different purpose) cite an idea to which he had formerly given expression, so under "the guidance and sanction of the Holy Spirit," as Dr. Blaikie admits, "the New Testament writers did make the modifications, on the ground that they conveyed the spirit and substance of the passages in a form perhaps better adapted to their immediate purpose."

The Divine Author of Scripture had doubtless important ends to serve in thus guiding inspired writers in making such deviations from the original. "Some of the deviations," says Dr. Fairbairn, "are chiefly to be regarded as notes of time, and on that account serve an important purpose (as in Deut. v. compared with Exod. xx., showing the former to have been meant to be a substantial, though not slavish rehearsal of the latter). Others may be regarded as proofs of the individuality of the writers—itself also in certain respects a matter of considerable importance—and of their desire to bring out some specific shades of meaning, which might otherwise have been overlooked. Many of them find their solution in the change of circumstances which rendered a sort of explanatory or paraphrastic rendering of the original advisable and proper. And while nothing in respect to doctrine or duty is ever built on the variations introduced into passages, subsequently employed or quoted, while often the greatest stress in those respects is laid upon the precise words of the original, the freedom thus manifested in the handling of Scripture is itself fraught with an important lesson, serving as a kind of protest against the rigid formalism and superstitious regard for the letter, which prevailed among the rabbinical Jews. Unlike these, the New Testament writers always exhibit the deepest and most correct insight into the spirit and design of the Old Testament passages they refer to, even when showing an apparent disregard of the precise form. They showed, as Auberlen remarks, that they knew how to read, as well as to write Scripture. So that, when the matter is fully considered, and weighed in all its bearings, there is nothing in it that militates against the doctrine of the plenary inspiration of Scripture." (*Bible Dictionary*, p. 791.)

Dr. Blaikie says, that "Whatever alterations, therefore, the inspired writers of the New Testament made must be held to have been within the true scope of the passages, and in harmony with the view of inspiration held by those to whom they were writing. They were not bound to the *ipsissima verba*." Why should they be bound to the *ipsissima verba*, or who affirms that they were? "Where the Spirit of the Lord is, there is liberty." He is surely as free as any merely human author to convey, through inspired writers, the same truth, in a slightly altered form of expression, better adapted to another context. Dr. Blaikie says that "this recognized a certain flexibility in the original words not consistent with the rigid doctrine of inspiration." If affirming, as we do, that "all statements of the original Scriptures are true in the sense divinely intended," "is the rigid doctrine of inspiration" here referred to, I fail to see how the modification in the New Testament of the phraseology of any passage quoted from the Old is inconsistent therewith. I may cite any passage, even from another writer, so as to convey accurately his meaning, although I do not give the *ipsissima verba*, and much more can I do so when quoting from my own writings. I am simply amazed that Dr. Blaikie should regard the manner in which "quotations" are made from the Old Testament in the New, as any proof whatever, that there were "errors" in the Scriptures as originally given.

In point of fact, instead of being proof of "error," these

deviations from the *ipsissima verba* of the original, in the case of quotations from the Old Testament made in the New, are seen, when rightly understood, to afford the strongest possible proof that the Old and New Testaments alike had, in all their parts, *one Divine Author*, whatever the variety of their human authorship. When I quote from the writings of another author, I generally require to give his *ipsissima verba*, lest by using another form of words I should, to any extent, misrepresent his meaning. But when I quote from my own writings I may freely give expression to my meaning in a *different form of words*.

Even so, the *ipsissima verba* of the Old Testament are not always used in New Testament quotations, just because this is a case in which the Divine Author is anew giving expression to the same truth in different words.

And this argument, in favour of the one Divine authorship of the Bible, becomes specially strong, when we take into account the almost superstitious veneration of the Jews for the letter of the Old Testament. No Jew would have ventured to quote in the New Testament, in a form different from the original, any passage of the Old Testament, unless in so doing he was acting under that Divine infallible guidance which is the essential element in inspiration.

Quotations are doubtless often made from the Septuagint on very purpose to show that the Bible, even in a translated form (so far as the true sense is given in the translation), is as much the Word of God as the original Scriptures. There are also variations in *form of expression* to show that while the letter of Scripture is of great importance, and arguments may be based on the use of single words, it is still more important that we perceive "the sense divinely intended."

The *third* and only other *argument* used by Dr. Blaikie in favour of the view that there were "errors" in the Scriptures, as originally given, is based on so-called "discrepancies" of which three specimens are cited. It so happens that in the letters to myself three specimens were also given. Two of these were the same as those adduced in the Letter to Dr. Bonar, viz., the two versions of the Decalogue, and Stephen's so-called "discrepancy" about the sepulchre. In the letter to me, instead of the inscription on the Cross, the lists in Ezra and Nehemiah of those who returned from Babylon, were cited.

It is really amusing to see within what small compass the so-called "discrepancies" or "errors" are compressed, when we ask for instances. After the merriment created throughout the country by the specimen given by Dr. Dods of "the Centurion" (even as, forty years ago, it had been given by M. Sherer), and after the conclusive and crushing reply in regard to it of Count Gasparin of Geneva, we shall surely have no further reference made to that specimen.

As my two appended letters fully discuss the alleged "discrepancies" in the two versions of the Decalogue and the speech of Stephen, I care not to repeat myself. Dr. Fairbairn, referring to the former case, says—"*There has been given to the Decalogue a double record,* first in Exodus xx. 2-17, again in Deuteronomy v. 6-21; and there are certain differences between the two forms, which have been taken advantage of by rationalistic interpreters, sometimes for the purpose of disparaging the historical correctness of either form, and sometimes as a conclusive argument against the doctrine of plenary inspiration." I wonder what Dr. Fairbairn would have said if he had found "interpreters" such as he refers to occupying Free Church Theological Chairs.

After specifying the differences between the two versions of the Decalogue, Dr. Fairbairn goes on to say—"It is obvious that these differences leave the main body or substance of the Decalogue, as a revelation of law, entirely untouched; not one of them affects the import and bearing of a single precept; nor, if viewed in their historical relation, can they be regarded as involving in any doubt or uncertainty the verbal accuracy of the form presented in Exodus. We have no reason to doubt that the words there recorded are precisely those which were uttered from Sinai, and written upon the table of stone. In Deuteronomy Moses gives a revised account of the transactions, using throughout certain freedoms, as speaking in a hortative manner, and from a more distant point of view; and, while he repeats the commandments as those which the Lord had spoken from the midst of the fire and written on tables of stone, Deut, v. 22, he yet shows, in his very mode of doing it, that he did not aim at an exact reproduction of the past, but wished to preserve to some extent the form of a free rehearsal. This especially appears in the addition to the fifth commandment, 'as the Lord thy God commanded thee,' which distinctly pointed back to a prior original, and even recognized that as the permanently existing form. The introducing also of so many of the later commands with the copulative *and*, tends to the same result; as it is precisely what would be natural in a rehearsal, though not in the original announcements, and came from combining with the legislative something of the narrative style. Such being plainly the character of this later edition, its other and more noticeable deviations—the occasional amplifications admitted into it, the substitution of *desire* for *covet*, with respect to a neighbour's wife, in the tenth command; and of the deliverance of Israel from Egypt, for the divine order of procedure at the creation, in the fourth—fall to be regarded as slightly varied and explanatory statements, which it was perfectly competent for the authorized mediator of the covenant to introduce, and which, in nature and design, do not materially differ from the alterations sometimes made by inspired writers of the New Testament on the passages they quote from the Old. They are not without use in an exegetical respect; and in the present case have also a distinct historical value, from the important evidence they yield in favour of the Mosaic authorship of Deuteronomy; since it is inconceivable that any later author, fictitiously personating Moses, would have ventured on making such alterations on what had been so expressly ascribed by Moses to God Himself, and which seemed to bear on it such peculiar marks of sacredness and inviolability." (*Bible Dictionary*, pp. 423-4.)

If, as Dr. Fairbairn argues, it was competent for Moses to make the variations in a hortative discourse, delivered many years after the events at Sinai, on the plains of Moab, surely we have in the *faithful* record of the variations thus introduced by Moses, one of the strongest possible proofs of the inspiration of the author of Deuteronomy. An uninspired writer, knowing as he must have done the version of the Decalogue in the earlier record of Exodus, would have been under strong temptation to give precisely the very same words, and attribute them to Moses. That would specially have been the case, if, as the higher critics would have us believe, Deuteronomy was written not by Moses, but by some author personating Moses centuries afterwards.

Thus, the author of Deuteronomy, whoever he was, and whatever the date of the book, gives the most incontrovertible proof of the truthfulness of his report of the speech of Moses on the plains of Moab. Although he knew of the earlier form of the Decalogue, he faithfully records the variations made by Moses in his speech, notwithstanding that he must have been conscious that they might become, in subsequent ages, a stumbling block to "rationalistic interpreters." So far, therefore, from this being a case of proved "error" in the original Scriptures, the function of inspiration in securing *truthfulness*, in the case of reported speeches, is by it most strikingly verified.

And the same thing is true in the case of the speech of Stephen. "Ludovicus" (referred to p. 48), says in his letter to the *Glasgow Herald* :—" The passage (Acts vii. 16) may be paraphrased as follows :—' Jacob died, he and our fathers, and they (our fathers) were carried over to Sychem and buried, he (Jacob) in the sepulchre which Abraham bought for a sum of money ; and they (the other patriarchs) in that of the sons of Emmor, the father of Sychem.' That rendering removes the difficulty, or we can say with the great Bochart that some unskilful grammarian, thinking that a nominative case was wanting before the verb ὠνήσατο, *was bought*, wrote in the margin the word *Abraham*, which others inserted into the text, without which the passage would run thus, and that with exact truth, ' So Jacob went down into Egypt and died' (there) ' he and our fathers ; and they,' (our fathers) ' were carried over into Sychem, and laid in the sepulchre that was bought for a sum of money of the sons of Emmor, the father of Shechem.'" If that single word *Abraham* had been interpolated in the way indicated, every one of the four so-called "discrepancies" found by Dr. Blaikie in this single passage, as compared with the account in Genesis, would forthwith disappear. It is true that neither that explanation, nor the other suggested by "Ludovicus," would dispose of the difficulty raised by Dr.

Blaikie (when referring to the view of Turretine), viz., that no mention is made in the Old Testament of the patriarchs being buried at Shechem. That difficulty, however, is easily disposed of, if we only remember that, as Dr. Blaikie contends, "'presumption' is not a trustworthy support." It is a case of mere "presumption" when Dr. Blaikie argues that, "had the bones of his brothers been taken too, mention would surely have been made of it," because "it is said that Joseph's bones were carried up."

But while either of the explanations given by "Ludovicus" may meet the difficulty, I repeat what I said in my letter to Dr. Blaikie, viz., that my view, as to the function of inspiration, in the case of reported speeches, is verified, if we have in Acts a *truthful* account of what was actually said by Stephen. The testimony to the absolute *truthfulness* of the report in Acts is only the more striking even if Stephen actually made a mistake in his speech. Instead of correcting it as an uninspired reporter would probably have done, Luke, guided by the Spirit, faithfully records the words of Stephen as actually spoken. Will Dr. Blaikie affirm that Luke did not give a *truthful* report of the speech as delivered ?

The only remaining case of so-called "discrepancy," viz., that of the *fourfold account of the inscription upon the Cross*, is the favourite specimen adduced by the advocates of the view that there were errors in the Scriptures as originally given. This alleged "discrepancy" is easily explained, if it is only remembered that what we claim for the original Scriptures is that all their statements were "true in the sense divinely intended"; that "inspiration does not guarantee verbatim reporting any more than any other kind of reporting;" that we may have a truthful summary as well as a truthful verbatim report; that in the case of each Gospel, the inscription is referred to in a different manner; that it was written, as we are expressly told, in three different languages, and may have been somewhat differently given in each language; that each of the inspired Evangelists was guided so to give his account as to bring out the greatest variety of detail, and thus to make it abundantly manifest that there was no collusion among the witnesses. Dr. Blaikie says that "the precise words of the inscription must have been present to the Holy Ghost," and asks, "If the words of Scripture are as much the words of God as the words of man, why were they not then, in all the four cases, accurately reproduced?" Here is an illustration of that strange confusion of thought on the part of Dr. Blaikie to which I have already referred. The words upon the Cross were not "*the words* of God," but the words of Pilate. Further, the inscription was written in letters of Latin, and of Hebrew, as well as of Greek, and so, if by accurate reproduction is meant reproduction of the *ipsissima verba*, these three languages must have been reproduced in each Gospel in their distinctive characters. As the object of the inscription was to make known the crime charged against the Crucified One, it is noteworthy that in each account we find the words, "The King of the Jews." But while this essential element was found in Greek, and Latin, and Hebrew, so as to be understood by the different nationalities who spoke these languages, is there, in view of all the circumstances, anything improbable in the supposition made by Dr. Geikie, that what was added to these words varied in each language, and that the full inscription as it appeared to the beholders may have taken such a triple form as the following:—

ישוע הנצרי מלך היהודים
Οὗτός ἐστιν Ἰησοῦς ὁ βασιλεὺς τῶν Ἰουδαίων.
Rex Judæorum.

Supposing that the inscription assumed such varied forms in the three languages, what becomes of Dr. Blaikie's charge of inaccuracy against three of the evangelists (for if valid, it must be made against three at least out of the four). But apart from all this, there is the further fact that no two of the evangelists profess to quote exactly the same thing in the Greek (in which the Gospels were written), into which the Hebrew and Latin forms of the inscription had to be translated. Matthew professes to give—τὴν αἰτίαν αὐτοῦ; Mark—ἐπιγραφὴ τῆς αἰτίας αὐτοῦ; Luke—ἐπιγραφὴ; John—τίτλον. (See Appendix III.) Each account is "true in the sense divinely intended." Each gives either a different part or a different version of the inscription. Each account supplements the others. And in all this we see one of the most striking proofs of an infallible Divine guidance; for every one must feel that, for the grand purpose of assuring us of historic credibility and truthfulness, it was better that we have four independent accounts, each supplementing the other, than that we have the same *verbatim* account by each evangelist—involving, as it would, writing down the letters of three different languages—if we were to get the whole of the *ipsissima verba* used by Pilate.

I have now disposed of all the arguments cited by Dr. Blaikie, in support of his view that there were errors in the Scriptures as originally given, and have shown that, instead of there being "error," each case, when properly understood, supplies new evidence that all the statements of the original Scriptures are " true in the sense divinely intended: that sense being also consistent with a fair use of words, within the range of legitimate human speech." I am amazed that one with the pronounced evangelical views of Dr. Blaikie should seek, on the basis of such " phenomena," to set aside the many statements of Scripture writers regarding their own writings, and to contradict the testimony of our Lord and His Apostles as to " the infallible truth and Divine authority " of Holy Scripture in all its statements—its statements of fact as well as of doctrine and duty.

Dr. Blaikie is ever reiterating the assertion that, as opposed to the deductive method, he inducts his view of inspiration from the statements and facts of Scripture. He charges us, moreover, with doing something else—with proceeding upon "'presumption,' which is not a trustworthy support." As I have already told him, he is utterly mistaken on this point. We do not, as he still insinuates, argue from any such " presumption " as he cites from Dr. Cunningham. We have no " *a priori* theory " on the subject of inspiration. We hold that it is " presumption " on his part to quote the words of Dr. Cunningham and to assume, without any proof, that we endorse them. We go to the statements and facts of Scripture, as Dr. Blaikie professes to do, but fails to do, and from these we induct our doctrine of inspiration. We agree with him that:—"By Protestants the true doctrine of inspiration must be inducted from the Word of God, and from that alone. It must be derived from a fair, candid, comprehensive view both of the statements of Scripture and of the phenomena of Scripture."

But we object to "the view both of the statements of Scripture and of the phenomena of Scripture" given by Dr. Blaikie, because it is neither "fair," nor "candid," nor "comprehensive."

How does the case stand as regards the statements of Scripture? Dr. Blaikie is constrained to make the following admissions on that point:—"There can be no manner of doubt that again and again the Scriptures claim to be the Word of God; they assert that in time past God spake to the fathers by the prophets; they affirm that the Holy Ghost spake by David and other writers of Scripture; that all Scripture is given by inspiration of God; and in reference to the New Testament, the Apostle Paul claims that he taught not in the words which man's wisdom teacheth, but which the Holy Ghost teacheth." He might have greatly added to the list of such testimonies, as, for instance, when Peter says that "holy men of God spake as they were moved by the Holy Ghost," and classed the writings of Paul with "the other Scriptures." But there is one testimony which Dr. Blaikie entirely overlooks, in the body of his letter to Dr. Bonar. I refer to the testimony of our Lord—to the manner in which He ever appeals to all parts of the Old Testament Scriptures as authoritative and true. And He thus refers to all classes of facts as infallibly true—not only to doctrinal facts, and to great historical facts, but also to incidental circumstances and facts of apparently minor importance, and even to incidents that have formed the chief stumbling-blocks to infidels, as when He endorses the fact that Jonah was three days in the whale's belly. Nor is this all. While He thus endorses as infallibly true numerous details of the Old Testament, He uses the all-comprehensive expression:—"And the Scripture cannot be broken"—a statement all the more emphatic, because introduced in support of an argument based on a single word in one of the Psalms.

To His testimony, so conclusive as to the infallibility of Scripture, in its statements of fact as well as of doctrine and duty, there is ample reference under the fourth head of our "Statement" on the case of Dr. Dods. And yet Dr. Blaikie does not make a single reference to what is there said. His only reference to the testimony of our Lord is in Appendix I., where he says: " I do not forget here how our Lord and His Apostles, in quoting from the Old Testament, sometimes made their argument turn on particular words or forms of words. This, I think, is the strongest point in your position. It undoubtedly ought to have most earnest attention in any comprehensive endeavour to induct a doctrine of inspiration. But in all fairness it ought to be considered alongside the other practice of which I have been speaking. Our business must be to harmonize the two practices. We should seek for some common ground on which to justify both. Perhaps there may be something peculiar to the passages which were used as verbal arguments. This is one of the difficulties of the subject, regarding which brethren on both sides should be more ready to help each other than to run their opponents up into a corner and prove them heretics." These are striking admissions. Evidently Dr. Blaikie feels " that he is run up into a corner," when the direct affirmations of the Lord Jesus Christ, to the contrary, are cited against his own unproved inference as to there being "errors" in the Scriptures as originally given. A little more regard for His authority, His infallibility—for if Divine He must be infallible—might surely have led Dr. Blaikie to consider prayerfully whether there might not be some explanation of the use of " Pre-existing Documents "; of " Quotations "; and of the three cases of so-called " discrepancy " cited, which would have obviated the necessity for his directly contradicting the testimony of our Lord. As will be seen from my letters, I have already done my best to help him on this point, but, instead of being publicly thanked for my pains, he accuses me of being " combative " when I might be " conciliatory "; of running him " up into a corner "; and of seeking to prove him a heretic!

It was wont to be regarded as the duty of our Theological Professors to seek, in the use of a little sanctified common sense and under the teaching of the Divine Spirit, to clear up any difficulties that might present themselves in the interpretation of the Sacred Scriptures, on the understanding that all statements of the original Scripture were " true in the sense divinely intended." But it seems that nowadays our Professors have come to the conclusion that they best discharge their duty to the Church and to her future ministers, and that they best fulfil their ordination vows, by seeking to demonstrate that there were "errors" in the Scriptures as originally given, and by holding up to ridicule as "like the maunderings of an imbecile," any attempted explanation of difficulties. From the manner in which Dr. Blaikie refers to the matter one would conclude that no explanations have been suggested except such as involve "torturing Scripture," and are "worthy neither of consideration nor respect."

I wonder that Dr. Blaikie, even if he thought it fair to suppress all other explanations, was not ashamed to use such "intemperate" language regarding the only one to which he refers (Turretine's), suggested, as it was, by a man probably as learned as himself. He might have remembered that whether that explanation was satisfactory or not, it was at least offered by one who was impressed, on the one hand, by the fact that, Scripture writers claim infallibility for their own writings, and that Christ endorsed that claim; on the other, by the fact that (to use the words of Farrar, who cannot be accused of holding a "rigid view of inspiration,") neither "the widest learning" nor "the acutest ingenuity of scepticism" has "ever pointed to one complete and demonstrable error of fact or doctrine in the Old or New Testament." Dr. Blaikie, merely because he has not yet come across any explanation of these three cases, which he regards as satisfactory, is "irreverent" enough to treat them all as cases of proved "discrepancy" or "error" in the Scriptures as originally given—notwithstanding the claims to infallibility for these Scriptures made by Biblical writers, and the endorsation of these claims by Christ Himself. When he thinks that he is at liberty, notwithstanding his ordination vows, thus to contradict the plain statements of Scripture and of the Confession of Faith, as also the testimony of our Lord, I am surprised that he ventures to speculate as to the possible comments of Pascal on the conduct of his opponents on this question (Appendix IV.). And my surprise is increased, when I find that Dr. Blaikie supposes that in a Book constructed as the Bible is, with its doctrines and duties resting on a groundwork of history—a Book which is one homogeneous whole—it is possible, somehow or other, to dissociate the doctrines and duties from the facts, and to hold that the former may be infallibly true and of Divine authority, while the latter may be erroneous to a greater or less extent. He tries to quiet our fears as to the baneful effects of the views for which he contends by saying that :—" The toleration asked is practically limited to matters that are subordinate and incidental; it does not extend to the great verities of revelation. It is connected with the structure rather than the substance of the Scripture. It in no degree invalidates the truth and preciousness of the grand testimony :—' This is the record, that God hath given to us eternal life, and this life is in His Son.'" I am at a loss to know how Dr. Blaikie could have penned such words, and attempted thus to draw a distinction between "structure" and "substance," between what is "subordinate and incidental," and "the great verities of revelation." No such distinction is recognized in the Confession of Faith. More important still, no such distinction is recognized in Scripture itself, or in the testimony of our Lord and His Apostles regarding Scripture. In the lexicon now lying on my table "verity" is explained as meaning "truth, consonance of a statement, proposition, or other thing to fact; a true assertion." In these senses, *all* the statements of Scripture are declared to be "verities" in the Confession of Faith, in the Scriptures, and by our Lord and His Apostles. If Scripture is not to be believed, when it refers to so-called "incidental and subordinate" matters, we instinctively feel that its testimony regarding "the great verities of revelation" is forthwith shaken. In that case, "the grand testimony:—'This is the record, that God hath given to us eternal life, and this life is in His Son,'" is assuredly invalidated, whatever Dr. Blaikie asserts to the contrary.

If I discover that in earthly things—the things which I can verify—inspired writers do not speak the truth, how can I trust them, when they speak to me of heavenly things? Is it not precisely, in this very way, that, in courts of law, the testimony of important witnesses is invalidated on cross-examination by skilled advocates? If it can be proved that the witness has not spoken the truth in regard to minor matters, the advocate is not slow to impress that fact upon the jury, with the view of invalidating his evidence in chief. And so it is in regard to Holy Scripture. These so-called "incidental and subordinate" matters, instead of being, as Drs. Dods and Blaikie try to persuade themselves, of "no real importance," are often of the greatest possible importance, as a means of confirming our faith in the "grand testimony" of the Bible regarding the "great verities of revelation." To quote once more the language of Dr. Fairbairn, "They connect the writer with the times and circumstances in which he lived. They were so many points of contact between himself and the living world around him; and points that often form a kind of bridge between the sacred and the profane territory; in the first instance, giving an air of naturalness and verisimilitude to the revelation, and afterwards supplying *data* for the verification of its contents. How much should the Bible have wanted in general interest and appearance of truthfulness, if it were stripped of the minor details which are found in it? And how many incidental confirmations of its genuineness and authenticity should have been lost, which, mainly in connection with these notices of common affairs, have been furnished by later research? It is to them, in great measure we owe the possibility of such works as Paley's *Horæ Paulinæ*, Smith's *Narrative of Paul's Shipwreck*, and many similar works, which have rendered the most essential service to the defence of the Bible. The genealogies themselves have their value; for they are, in a manner, the skeletons of history, on whose naked ribs, or projecting outlines, we can often grope our way to interesting or important movements in the past. And, besides the more special lessons which it will always be found on careful reflection can be derived from the mention of things comparatively little and common, there is this instructive lesson—that the Book, which is emphatically the revelation of God's mind to men, does not disdain to touch on even the smaller matters that concern them, and while it seeks to lift them above earthly and sensuous things, still willingly accords to these the place that properly belongs to them." As even Dr. Blaikie is constrained to admit that "in whatever manner the historical records of the Old Testament may have been compiled, they are marvels of accuracy"; and that "all the information recently gathered from the cuneiform inscriptions and other monuments of antiquity attests this fact," he ought not to make reckless charges against the Bible, which, to his confusion, may be promptly disproved by further discoveries of "cuneiform inscriptions and other monuments of antiquity."

In the "Statement" on which Dr. Blaikie animadverts, we ask for information as to "how and where the dividing line is to be drawn between the true and the erroneous," if there were errors in the original Scriptures. But he gives no reply to such an inquiry. He cannot controvert the affirmation we make, that we "should require a new revelation to enable us to draw such a distinction," and that "without such a new revelation there would, according to this theory, be no clear, fixed, objective standard of doctrine and duty." He cannot deny that, if his view were correct, " the critic would be largely dependent upon his own spiritual consciousness, his own whims and caprices, for a knowledge of what is of infallible truth and divine authority in the Scriptures"; and that "for the same knowledge the great mass of the people would be as dependent upon the critics as they are upon priests under the régime of the Church of Rome."

He does not attempt to answer the question we put:—"What guarantee could any one have that the critics, especially when they differ so much among themselves as to what are to be regarded as errors, could be implicitly trusted, when thus sitting in judgment upon the original document—each one, according to his own theological standpoint, drawing for himself the dividing line between the true and the false in the Bible —getting rid by this theory not only of such facts as he does not care to believe, but also of such doctrines as do not commend themselves to his acceptance?" Instead of doing this, it is noteworthy that even when Dr. Blaikie speaks of matters that are "subordinate and incidental," all the length he goes is to say that the toleration asked is "*practically limited*" to these. Even if he or any one else had been able strictly to define what is meant by matters that are "subordinate and incidental," it turns out that the toleration asked for is not to be limited *exclusively* to these, as the Report of the College Sub-Committee led us to believe, but only "*practically.*" In other words, each member of the "forward movement" party is to be left free to determine for himself how much of the Bible he will set aside as erroneous, and where there is no principle to guide, it is certain that the practice would be very divergent. Dr. Blaikie tells us about his own practice. He says, "I have never seen cause to apply that hypothesis" (the hypothesis, viz., about pre-existing documents—uninspired and erroneous, yet endorsed by inspired writers,) "to the Book of Genesis, for example, to the extent to which it has been proposed to carry it." While we ought to be thankful that Dr. Blaikie has not yet seen cause to go as far as some others, will he kindly explain how, after he has defended his theory, and voted for unlimited license in its practical application, he can prevent those who adopt it—his own students for instance—from carrying it much further than he himself does, and from speaking, as some of the party are already doing, of the earlier chapters of the Book of Genesis, as a piece of "Babylonian mythology with a smack of Judaism"? Will he explain how, on his theory, he can resist the surrender of any portion whatever of the Old Testament or of the New? On the same principle, on which he regards himself as entitled to reject part of the Bible as fallible—to reject its testimony on matters that are "subordinate and incidental"—he may reject the whole. As Heber well puts it:—"It is the misfortune of this Scythian mode of warfare, that it is only suited to a territory which, like Scythia, is little worth preserving; and that the practice once begun of abandoning to the pursuer whatever parts of Scripture it does not exactly suit us to defend, no means of defence will at length remain for those tenets themselves which we now regard as of vital importance."

Dr. Dods and others flatter themselves that by such concessions they will conciliate infidels. The rejoinder of Huxley to the authors of *Lux Mundi*, shows how vain and illusory is such a hope. I challenge Dr. Blaikie, or any one else, to meet the argument of the Father of Dr. Dods on this point. Referring to the advantage supposed to be gained in dealing with the infidel, by adopting a theory in substance the same as that now advocated by Dr. Blaikie, he, 60 years ago, wrote as follows:—" Let us see then what advantage this gives us in dealing with the infidel. He lays his hand on a certain verse and says, Surely this cannot be inspired. I escape by saying, True, but then you see it is not of a religious or moral nature. His next question is, What are the parts of the Bible which are inspired? and how do you distinguish them from those parts which, not being religious, are not inspired? To answer this, I call in the aid of the learned, the wise, and the good, who have maintained this view. I seek in them for some general rule, some fixed and well established principle, by which I may separate what is human from what is Divine in the Bible. But my search is vain. I find no such rule or principle. On the contrary, it is obvious that no two men will answer it precisely in the same way. The only advantage then that I derive from this low view, is to enable the infidel to wedge me into a difficulty from which there is no possibility of escape.

" But even supposing this unanswerable question to be answered, I can derive no advantage from it. For the infidel lays his hand upon a verse which I acknowledge to be of a religious nature, and says, This is very oddly expressed. I must not say with the apostle, 'We speak not the words which man's wisdom teacheth, but which the Holy Ghost teacheth,' nor observe that it is nothing wonderful, if the wisdom of God should sometimes appear foolishness to man; but I must say, The expression may be awkward; I defend not the expression, but the sentiment. But should he reply, If the expression be a human and an awkward expression, how can you convince me that the sentiment is not the same? I confess I know not what I should say. And should he go on to observe, that as the sacred writers often assert their own inspiration—the inspiration of ALL Scripture, if we admit that in not a few instances they really were *not* inspired, we must of necessity conclude, that in point of fact they were *never* inspired, I know not how I could resist the conclusion.

" Such are the advantages to be derived from seeking to

conciliate the infidel by concession—a principle which I regret to see creeping into some of our best Theological Treatises of late. If the Scriptures are spurned by the infidel, when they are presented to him as wholly the Word of God, it is preposterous to suppose that they will command his reverence when presented to him as partly the Word of God and partly that of man,—as 'a motley collection, composed partly under the inspiration of *suggestion,* partly under the inspiration of *elevation,* partly under the inspiration of *superintendence,* and partly under no inspiration at all !' Give the infidel one book or one verse, and upon the same principle he has a right to demand the surrender of the whole Bible."

Thus far I have dealt only with the question of "errors" in the original Scriptures. But there remains the further question about the term "immoralities," applied by Dr. Dods to what is "commended. or even commanded" in the Old Testament. On this point Dr. Blaikie said nothing in his letters to myself, and therefore I am the more startled when, from his Letter to Dr. Bonar, I find that here also, he has become an eager apologist for the view of Dr. Dods. The use of the term "immoralities," as applicable to what is "commended, or even commanded" in the Old Testament has been so universally condemned even by the supporters of Dr. Dods, that the compilers of the "Statement" did not think it necessary to amplify on that point. In our simplicity, we supposed that it had been left to the school of Voltaire, Paine, and Ingersoll, to denounce the morality of the Old Testament.

Indeed, I fully expected that, when Dr. Blaikie (with the views he personally holds about "errors" in the original Scriptures) sought to justify his action in voting for a motion which declares that the Church "views the use of the term 'mistakes and immoralities' to describe recognized difficulties in the Scriptures as utterly unwarranted, and fitted to give grave offence," he would have called attention to the fact that the deliverance does not use the phrase "*mistakes or immoralities,*" but "*mistakes and immoralities,*" and that he would have said that he voted for it, because, while he believed that there were "mistakes" in the original Scriptures, he did not believe that there were "immoralities." But in this, it seems I was mistaken. It turns out that Dr. Blaikie defends the use by Dr. Dods of each term separately and singly. He not only apologizes for the use of this most offensive term, "immoralities," but even like Dr. Dods uses "intemperate" language, with the view of pouring contempt on those who do not agree with him. He speaks of a "tendency" to "go into hysterics" over this matter " even in the deliverance of the Assembly."

After this, one scarcely knows what to expect from the present generation of theological Professors in the Free Church.

In my student days I was taught by Dr. Fairbairn to regard the morality of the Bible, of the Old and New Testaments alike, as one of the most conclusive proofs of its inspiration.

For what he had to say on that point, and for evidence of the manner in which he dealt with the objection raised by infidels against the morality of the Old Testament, I must refer to his article in *Bible Dictionary*, pp. 216-18. Referring to the objection taken by "adversaries" to the morality of the Bible, he says, "This can only be affirmed with the slightest degree of plausibility, when certain portions are isolated, and considered out of their proper bearing and connection, or when the statements it contains are represented in a false and distorted light." Dr. Blaikie affirms that there are "very strange points in the morality of the Old Testament," and that "it is a delicate task to reconcile Old Testament morality in some points with the inspiration of Scripture." When this is the kind of teaching about Scripture given to our future ministers, and when Dr. Dods speaks of "immoralities" as "commended, or even commanded" in the Old Testament, we have "need to fall on our knees," in shame and confusion of face, before the Holy One whose character is being thus aspersed.

On the supposition that the Old Testament is the Word of God, or even on the supposition that it contains a truthful historical record of Divine commands, the words used by Dr. Dods are a charge made, not against the Bible, but against God. On that supposition, the charge of immorality is made, not against the Book which records the command, but against Him who issued the command. The blasphemy, involved in such a charge against Him, is simply revolting. If any thing "commanded" in the Old Testament was immoral, Dr.

Dods can only escape from bringing a charge of immorality against the Holy God—the Fount and Source of all Morality—by denying that the commands of the Old Testament came from Him, in other words, by denying the historical trust-worthiness, not to speak of the inspiration of the Old Testament. I am anxious to know on which horn of the dilemma Dr. Dods and his defender Dr. Blaikie choose to sit.

Dr. Blaikie says in his Letter to Dr. Bonar—" Perhaps you accept the view of a progressive revelation of morality." He may strike out the "perhaps" from the sentence. We do most cordially "accept the view of a progressive revelation of morality." I know of no one who does not accept it. That view was one of the commonplaces in my theological training. But I fail to see how, in accepting that view, I go "a great way," or even a single step, "to meet Dr. Dods." A "progressive revelation of morality"; a revelation such as the people were able to bear; a use of methods of moral instruction suited to a darker economy; these are very different things from the God of Holiness commanding "immoralities," just as a progressive revelation of truth, in which I also believe, is a very different thing from the God, "who is truth itself," revealing "error." As Dr. Fairbairn well puts it, " the fallacy of the objection," based upon the morality of the Old Testament as contrasted with that of the New, " lies in this, that it supposes what is fit and proper for the more advanced state must have equally been so for the immature ; it would insist upon the child being put upon precisely the same regimen as the full-grown man. In no age of the Church can God sanction or countenance sin : but He may be more or less severe, also more or less outward, in the methods He authorizes or adopts for checking and chastising sin, according to the state of privilege enjoyed by His people, and the circumstances in which the world is placed. This consideration, fairly apprehended and applied, will be found quite adequate to account for the differences which, in a moral respect, exist between the earlier and the later portions of Scripture." (*Bible Dictionary*, p. 796.)

If " the view of a progressive revelation of morality," so well stated by Dr. Fairbairn, is all that is contended for by Drs. Dods and Blaikie, they have both been singularly unfortunate as regards the manner, in which they have expressed themselves. When even Ingersoll is content to speak of the "imperfect morality" of the Old Testament, it does seem passing strange that Dr. Dods should speak of "immoralities," and that Dr. Blaikie should seek to justify him in using such language. In a conversation I had, at the time of the Assembly, with one of our ecclesiastical leaders, I asked him to tell me, in view of the decision just then given on the case of Dr. Dods, how far a Minister or Professor of the Church may now go, in the way of publicly affirming that there were "errors" or "immoralities" in the original Scriptures, before he would be taken under discipline? "That would depend upon circumstances," was the reply. Thereafter, he volunteered the statement that he "had allowed Dr. Dods to get off this time, because he found that he did not use words in the same sense as other people." He had asked Dr. Dods what he meant by the term "mistakes and immoralities" as applied to Scripture, and had received the reply that "the things referred to were such trifles that he (Dr. Dods) was ashamed to mention them." The leader in question further informed me that, on receiving this answer, he had replied, "If they are such trifles, why do you use such offensive words in connection with Holy Scripture?" The question thus put to Dr. Dods was certainly a pertinent one, and the answer given seems to have made the leader believe that Dr. Dods is not so far apart from his brethren as his "intemperate" language would seem to imply. It would surely be a great deal more satisfactory if, in view of all the anxieties Dr. Dods has awakened, he would take, not merely the leaders, but the Church as a whole, into his confidence, in making explanations. If he can conscientiously say anything that would tend to restore confidence; if he will explain when he does "use words in the same sense as other people;" if, by the term "immoralities," as applied to the Old Testament, he means simply that there was "a progressive revelation of morality" in the Bible, in the sense explained by Dr. Fairbairn, I, for one, would be glad to get even such an explanation. But if he has any regard to his own reputation, as one who can express his meaning clearly, he ought, in that case, manfully to withdraw the offensive word "immoralities," and to express his regret for having used it, and so given it currency among those who cavil at the Word of God, and will certainly use it in a very different sense. Such action on his part will be far more serviceable in removing misunderstandings and in promoting the peace and prosperity of the Church, than such an article as that written by him in the *British Weekly* of October 2, or such an ill-advised production as that now issued by Dr. Blaikie. In that article Dr. Dods not only, as already stated, holds up his brethren to scorn by describing them as "uninstructed Evangelicals, who have been combining with Secularists, Atheists, and anti-Christians in general, to betray the Christian position," but in the most unaccountable manner misrepresents their views in regard to the self-evidencing power of Christ. He says that, "Incalculable damage has been done, and is being done, by the modern evangelical abandonment of the ground taken by the Reformers, that Christ evidences Himself and the Scriptures also." I know of no one who has abandoned that doctrine of the Reformers. On the contrary, that is the very citadel of the impregnable fort we occupy, in defending the Word of God.

By the witnessing of the Spirit, in and with the Word, we have got in our hearts and lives experimental proof that Jesus Christ, of whom the Scriptures testify, is Divine, and that what He says of the Scriptures is true. Because we have such experimental evidence—evidence which always carries a conviction of certainty—we refuse, at the bidding of critics or Professors (who come to us with unproved assertions) to believe that there were "errors" or "immoralities" in the Scriptures as they came from Him, who is both True and Holy. We believe that, as shown by Dr. Dale, " the man who has evidence of Christ's power in his own heart and life is invulnerable by criticism."

But from the experimental evidence thus obtained, we draw a conclusion exactly the opposite of that drawn by Dr. Dods. His argument, as I understand it, is, "Christ evidences Himself and the Scripture also," therefore there were "errors" and "immoralities" in the Scriptures, as originally given. Our argument is, "Christ evidences Himself and the Scripture also," therefore critics and Professors are assuredly in the wrong when they contradict His testimony by declaring that there were "errors" in the Scriptures, as originally given by the God, "who is Truth itself," and that "immoralities" were "commended, or even commanded" in the Old Testament.

While I greatly admire the literary grace and charm of the Letter of Dr. Blaikie to Dr. Bonar (quite in keeping with his other productions, and showing that whatever his merits as a theologian, he at least excels as a *litteratcur*), I am painfully impressed with the weakness and inconclusive character of his argumentation. And in this, I do not stand alone. One ministerial friend described his production as "pitiably weak." Another spoke of it to me as a "new specimen of the 'feeble outpourings of Dr. Blaikie,'" using the language of the late Dr. Begg.

In my judgment the *weakness* of the production is due not to want of ability on the part of Dr. Blaikie. So far as that is concerned, he is qualified enough to be a leader in that "new forward movement" of which we hear so much nowadays. That is a movement led (so we are told) by men "skilled in all the learning of the Egyptians." Its aim is to emancipate the churches from that bondage to Scripture in which they have been so long held; to put an end to that "Bibliolatry," which has so long prevailed, and to conduct into a new "land of promise." Strange to say, the precise situation of the goodly land has not yet been clearly indicated, and many of us have looked in vain for any appearance of a guiding pillar. The only thing certain is, that when the land is reached there will be found inscribed, in large characters, upon its portal, the words :—" ERRORS " and " IMMORALITIES " in the ORIGINAL SCRIPTURES—a somewhat strange device, one would think, for a "land of promise." If any of the "obscurantists" or "uninstructed Evangelicals" will dare to oppose this "new forward movement" on the ground that, before advancing, they wish to get some more precise information as to its exact destination, and to get some assurance that there is a Divine command to advance in that direction, they are reminded of the fate that befell Pharaoh and his hosts in the Red Sea, and warned that, in an ecclesiastical sense, a similar fate will befall them.

Such being the nature of the "new forward movement," I am free to admit that Dr. Blaikie is quite qualified to take his place alongside of Drs. Dods and Bruce as one of its leaders. His Letter to Dr. Bonar shows that he can deftly handle his pen, and skilfully marshall his arguments, such as they are. Like a trained controversialist he can divert attention from the real question at issue, by misrepresenting the views of his opponents, and directing his artillery at men of straw. By well-known devices, such as by employing orthodox words and phrases (*e.g.* "Inspiration," "the Word of God," and even "an infallible objective revelation of the will of God," etc.), while he either limits their application, or evacuates them of their recognized meaning, he can throw the unwary off their guard, and make them believe that his deviations from the Standards of the Church are very slight. Nay, more, he can so misrepresent the past history of the Church, the past decisions of the Assembly, and the statements of the Confession, as to make it appear that the real innovators in this matter are those opposed to his peculiar views. In view of all these clever devices for concealing the flimsiness of the proof he adduces in support of his own opinions, no one is entitled to say that the weakness of his Letter to Dr. Bonar is due to want on his part of ability, scholarship, or dialectic skill.

It must be due to the essential "weakness" of the cause he seeks to defend. He has attempted *the impossible*, viz., to harmonize the Divine authorship of Scripture—"the Divine inspiration of the Holy Scriptures, of the whole of the Scriptures," with the view that there were "errors" and "immoralities" in these Scriptures as originally given by their Divine Author through inspired men. And in this he has signally failed, even as all must fail who make the same attempt.

He has tried to make it appear that the Bible is like Nebuchadnezzar's image—part of fine gold, part of silver, part of brass, part of iron, and part of clay. The only result has been, that it has been made abundantly manifest that the characteristics he applies to the Bible, belong not to it but to his own production. The Word of God, thrown into the crucible of his carping criticism, has come out, as it always will come out, when exposed to similar treatment, *all fine gold, seven times purified.*

As will be seen from my first letter, Dr. Blaikie exhorted me to keep to my proper sphere of work—a sphere for which he was good enough to tell me my "gifts fitted" me "so well and so exceptionally."

To what I have already said in reply, on that point, I must add a word in explanation of why I—an ordinary minister of the Church—who have taken some considerable share in home mission work, have been rash enough to cross swords with a learned Professor, even though at the risk of being ecclesiastically immolated for my temerity.

I regard the questions raised in this controversy as of *vital importance*, as bearing not only on my personal hopes of salvation, but also on the practical work of the Christian ministry, and on mission work in particular. In the suggestive life of Mackay, the hero of Uganda, the following statement occurs (p. 145):—" His bold and intelligent appeal to the Scriptures seems to have deeply impressed Mtesa, and this habit of referring all questions to the Word of God became in the end the chief factor in the mental and spiritual revolution which in the course of years passed over vast numbers of the Baganda."

Every one engaged in home mission work has a similar experience as to the absolute necessity of making constant appeal to the Word of God, if success is to be achieved. If I do not go to the careless and Christless as an ambassador of the King, clothed with His authority, and conveying His message—a message of "infallible truth and divine authority," because given by Him—they will despise my own words and opinions. They will tell me, and be justified in telling me, that their opinion is as good as mine. We who preach have a right to ask our hearers to believe and obey, because we declare unto them not the word of fallible men but the Word of God—the God " who is Truth itself."

Let a preacher begin to insinuate doubt on this point; let him tell the people that some of the statements of the Bible are, after all, *not true;* let him begin to draw fine distinctions between " structure " and " substance," between " matters that are subordinate and incidental" and "the great verities of revelation"—distinctions which are recognized neither in Scripture itself, nor in the testimony of Christ regarding Scripture—the only practical result will be, that his hearers will not only insist on excising from their Bibles the parts declared to be erroneous, but will refuse to believe what the preacher still professes, on the authority of the Bible, to regard as true. (See Appendix V.)

Sitting, as they haughtily do, in their "seats of learning"; looking down disdainfully "on obscurantists" and "un-instructed Evangelicals"; never coming into contact with the baneful effects among the common people of the reckless theories about Scripture they propagate and defend, our Professors may stigmatize as an "argument of unbelief" all we say in regard to the logical and practical outcome of their views, and may satisfy their own consciences by saying that all this is only a new proof that "it is quite possible that any concession on inspiration would be taken advantage of by some for illegitimate purposes." But I humbly submit that those who are conversant with the facts, and who bear "the burden and heat of the day," in the ordinary work of the ministry, and in home mission work, are as much entitled as are our Professors to have something to say on this subject. They have a right to insist that those who are regarded as representative men in the Church, and who are responsible for the training of her future ministers, shall not be at liberty, while subscribing the Church's Standards and receiving from her their support, to propagate views which tend to bring about such baneful results, or which at least are fitted to blunt the edge of "the sword of the Spirit, which is the Word of God."

APPENDIX I.

Pollokshields, 13*th June*, 1890.

Dear Dr. Blaikie,

I regret that yours of the 3rd inst. has been so long unanswered. I am sorry that one for whom I have so high a regard, and from whose published writings I have derived so much profit, should take exception to my views on Inspiration, and should come to the conclusion that I am leaving my proper sphere of work when I intermeddle with such subjects. I am specially mortified to find that after my former correspondence with you on this subject, and after I sent you my recently published Strictures on the Report of the College Committee, you do not seem even yet to understand my views. I have been at special pains to make it plain that I hold no theory as to the *mode* of inspiration, far less an "*a priori* theory," and least of all, what has been described as the "mechanical theory," or theory of "verbal dictation." Again and again I have stated that I concern myself simply with the *product* of inspiration, as declared in the Word of God and Confession of Faith, and as testified to by Christ and His Apostles, viz., a Book of "infallible truth and Divine authority." Notwithstanding all this, you still represent me as formulating "a theory of inspiration *a priori*."

In my published Strictures on the Report of the College Committee (p. 29), I make the following statement :—" The College Committee says that it 'includes men who abide deliberately and decidedly by what may be called the older view. They do not hold it as caricatured, whether by believing men like Alford, or by more sceptical opponents, but they hold that they have reason to believe all statements of the original Scriptures to be true, in the sense divinely intended : that sense being also consistent with a fair use of words within the range of legitimate human speech.' That I accept as a fair statement of the views of those now opposed to Dr. Dods, but instead of speaking of Alford as the one who caricatures, I would have substituted the names of certain ministers and professors of our own Church." To these words I still adhere. I cordially endorse the view as to the *product* of inspiration, thus described as "the older view"—not caricatured—said to be held by some of the members of the College Sub-committee. In the Assembly, I expressed my surprise, and I now again express my surprise that there should be a single member of that sub-Committee (and the words imply that there are several if not a majority of the whole) who does not see "reason to believe all statements of the original Scriptures to be true, in the sense divinely intended ; that sense being also consistent with a fair use of words within the range of legitimate human speech."

Am I to understand that you are one of that number ? Do you refuse to endorse that statement of personal belief ? You will observe that it has nothing to do with any "*a priori* theory of inspiration." It, however, has to do with the *product* of inspiration, and defines the sense in which all statements of the original Scriptures are believed to be true, viz., "the sense divinely intended : that sense being also consistent with a fair use of words within the range of legitimate human speech." Whatever be your own view, if you will only regard these words as giving a correct statement of the view I hold as to the *product* of inspiration, perhaps you will see that after all I can have little difficulty in showing that my view consists with the several cases of alleged "discrepancy" you cite.

The first case, that of the two versions of the Decalogue, is easily explained. The words recorded in Exodus, I regard as precisely those which were uttered from Sinai, and written upon the tables of stone. Those recorded in Deuteronomy purport to be part of a hortative speech delivered by Moses—a speech in which he uses throughout certain freedoms and makes certain amplifications. While he repeats the ten commandments as those which the Lord had spoken from the midst of the fire, and written on tables of stone, he shows plainly in his mode of doing so, that he did not aim at exact reproduction of the past, but wished to preserve to some extent the form of a free rehearsal. I refer you to what Dr. Fairbairn says on this point in his article on the Decalogue (Bible Dictionary, pp. 423-4).

If there is foundation for what Dr. Fairbairn says in that article, then the only question bearing on inspiration that can arise in regard to the Deuteronomic version of the Decalogue is:—Have we in Deuteronomy a *true* report of what was said by Moses to the people on the plains of Moab? If we have, then my view as to the product of inspiration is verified. Are you prepared to say that we have not a *true* report? When inspired writers report the sayings or doings of others, whether of good men or of bad men, or even of devils, I never understood that they were guided by the inspiring Spirit to correct the subject matter of what is reported. In all such cases I understood that inspiration secured *truthful* reporting—not necessarily verbatim reporting, but *truthful* reporting—for there may be a truthful summary, as well as a truthful verbatim report.

If in this case the words of Moses are truthfully reported in Deuteronomy, either *in extenso*, or in the form of a summary, in either case the statement is " true in the sense divinely intended."

The same principle I apply to the case you cite about Stephen's speech (Acts vii. 16). In an able letter of date March 29, 1890, signed "Ludovicus," which appeared in the *Glasgow Herald*, two possible explanations are given with the view of showing that the statement as originally made by Stephen was in harmony with the facts as recorded in Genesis. But even if it were otherwise, if it could be proved that Stephen in the course of his address had fallen into a mistake on this point, that would not give me any trouble with the view I take as to the province of inspiration in relation to reported speeches. The sole question I feel called upon to look at in that connection is:—Has the inspired historian Luke truthfully reported the speech of Stephen? Did Stephen really utter the words attributed to him in the original text of Acts? Are you prepared to say that he did not do so?

That chapter of Acts is intended to be—on its face it purports to be—a report of the speech of Stephen (whether *in extenso* or in abridged form is not stated), and if the report is " true in the sense divinely intended," even a mistake on the part of Stephen about the place of burial (a mistake, however, most unlikely in the circumstances) would give me no more trouble than do the mistaken views of Divine providence on the part of the friends of Job—mistakes corrected in the book in which they are recorded—or the lies of Satan which are truthfully reported (*e.g.*, temptation of our Lord), but are corrected by counter statements of divine truth.

As to the different lists in Ezra and Nehemiah of those who returned from Babylon, you have no right to assert that there is any "discrepancy" unless you are sure (1) that in each case the list was complete; (2) that each person had only one name; (3) that the lists were compiled at precisely the same time and referred to the same classes; and (4) that there was no corruption in either case of the original text.

The variations in the quotations from the Old Testament as made in the New have always seemed to me the most conclusive proof that could be adduced of the Divine Authorship of the Bible as a whole. If you, as a human author, may, in one part of a volume written by yourself, introduce the same idea in somewhat varied forms of expression, I really cannot understand why God should be restricted to the *ipsissima verba* of what has been formerly written under His own guidance. Is He not entitled through inspired men to give in the New Testament a somewhat different setting to any statement of the Old Testament, and to bring out more fully its hidden meaning?

I have looked into the passages of Calvin's Commentary to which you refer, and as I agree with what Calvin there says I am at a loss to know on what ground you represent me as casting "Calvin overboard."

You take credit to yourself for inducting your theory of inspiration from "the statements and the *facts* of Scripture," and your words imply that I do something else.

I also induct my views as to the *product* of inspiration from "the statements and *facts* of Scripture." I take into account, however, and attach chief importance to statements and facts, of which you seem to make no account whatever, viz.: the statements of the writers of Scripture regarding their own writings, and the writings of other inspired men, and very specially the testimony of Christ and His Apostles regarding Holy Scripture. You seem to me to ignore these most essential facts and you ask me to fix my attention exclusively on what you describe as "discrepancies" in our present Scriptures.

You take no account moreover of the fact—proved by the various readings—that there has been corruption to a greater or less extent of the original text, that mistakes of a trivial kind, none of them however affecting a single doctrine or duty revealed in the Bible, have been introduced through transcription, mistakes which are being eliminated as older MSS. are discovered. You insist that the discrepancies you think you have discovered in our present Bible must have been in the original document, although such an assertion cannot be proved.

Are you entitled in this way to use the facts of our present Bible?

Apply the same principle of reasoning to the Parable of the Tares. You go at the harvest time to the field in which the wheat and the tares are growing together, and from the *facts* you induct the theory that the owner of the field sowed tares as well as wheat. But you know that in that case your induction would be wrong, for an enemy sowed the tares and they were sown subsequently to the wheat. Or to take another illustration. You look at the facts of human nature as it now is. You hold God responsible for the wickedness now found in man. You know that you cannot reason thus, for in so doing you would contradict the statement of Scripture that "God made man upright," and at the same time you would deny the fact of the fall. I hold that you have as little warrant even if you do find "errors" or "discrepancies" in the present Scriptures for saying that they were in the Scriptures as originally given.

If, by a comparison of the best MSS. our higher critics can show that any statement of our present Scriptures had no place in the original text, I at once accept that result of their labours, and do not claim infallibility for any such interpolation. In all such cases, however, they must produce the objective authority of MSS., which is a different thing from the inner consciousness accepting or rejecting at pleasure what is found in the original text, on the ground that it contains a mixture of truth and error. In the one case there is a fixed objective standard, but in the other there is none. The relation of the individual to the Bible is different in the two cases. In the former case I accept the evidence of MSS. and bow before the authority of the Word of God. In the latter case the Divine communications are all subject to me. I am their master; I receive them only in so far as they commend themselves to my spiritual consciousness. Instead of bringing the facts of my spiritual experience to the Bible as to a fixed standard outside of me, for determining their quality, I bring the Bible to my spiritual experience, that I may find out how much of it I shall accept, and how much of it I shall reject.

You exhort me to keep to my proper sphere of work, and hint that I have not gifts fitting me for dealing with these questions of higher criticism, which our learned professors claim as specially belonging to them. From the manner in which you address me on this point, I suppose that you must, with Professor Drummond (see *British Weekly* of this week) class me among the "obscurantists."

Well, if our professors will keep their speculations to themselves,

I shall not presume to enter into controversy with men so superior in gifts and attainments. When, however, they insist on proclaiming in season and out of season, that there are "mistakes," "inaccuracies," "discrepancies," "errors," "immoralities," in the original Scriptures, thus doing their best to neutralize my testimony, and to defeat all the ends of the Christian ministry, I feel that I am not only entitled, but bound to do my best in the use of the powers God has given me, to vindicate the infallible truth and Divine authority of Scripture as taught in the Word of God and in the Confession, and as attested by Christ and His Apostles. Humble though my powers may be, I cannot forget that the Bible lies at the foundation of all my preaching and of all my personal hopes; that it is a book, not merely for higher critics, but for the common people, and that through the enlightening Spirit by whom it was inspired, things in it which are hid from "the wise and prudent" may be "revealed unto babes."

From your many writings, I know that you sympathize with evangelistic work in every form, and I cannot but believe that if you only knew the baneful effects that have already resulted from the utterances of Dr. Dods as to there being "errors" and "immoralities" in the original Scriptures, you would hesitate before seeking to vindicate him in making such statements. Your letter seems to imply that you wish to identify yourself with him in making these offensive statements. I hope that in this I misunderstand you, for in view of your evangelical standpoint, and the wholesome warning given in your recent admirable article on "The Old Pulpit and the New," I find it hard to persuade myself that this is your real position. The less am I able to do so when I find from the Division List that you supported the motion of Dr. Adam, which declared that the Assembly "views the use of the term 'mistakes and immoralities' to describe recognized difficulties in the Scriptures as utterly unwarranted, and fitted to give grave offence."

It seems to me that you are fighting a man of straw known as the "mechanical theory of inspiration," or the "theory of verbal dictation." This is plain from the fact that in an article recently contributed by you to an American newspaper, and reproduced in this country, you tried to persuade the American churches that those opposed to Dr. Dods are contending for "verbal dictation." After my previous correspondence with you, is this fair? On 10th May, 1878, you sent me a letter in which, after explaining, as you do now, that you follow the induction method, you said:—"It leads me to question the doctrine of verbal inspiration, at least as a universal phenomenon." On 19th February, 1880, you again wrote me to say that if you were writing over again the letter from which that extract is taken you would " alter one expression," and you added—" I do believe in the doctrine of verbal *inspiration ;* what I cannot receive is, the doctrine of verbal *dictation.*" On the day following I wrote you, enclosing a second time a copy of my Published Speech in the former case against Dr. Dods, and referred you to page 13 for proof that equally with yourself I repudiated " verbal dictation," which I regard as another name for the " mechanical theory of inspiration." After that correspondence, it seems to me unaccountable that you should regard yourself as entitled to write your recent article, misrepresenting so flagrantly to the American churches the real question at issue in this controversy.

I have always cherished the hope that, on getting into closer conference with each other, we would discover that after all there is not so great a divergence of view between the two parties in that controversy as at present appears, and hence my proposal for the appointment of a committee in the case of Dr. Dods. That proposal was, however, rejected, as was also a proposal I privately made to Dr. Rainy that the opening statement in the motion of Dr. Adam should be omitted. It seems to me to declare that the affirmations that there were " errors " in the original Scriptures, and that " immoralities " are " commended, or even commanded " in the Old Testament, are not " at variance with the standards of the Church," and consequently that no minister or professor can be cast out of the Church whatever lengths he may go in making such offensive statements. It seems that nothing else would satisfy Dr. Dods and his friends but to have in this manner a distinct reversal of the decision of the Assembly of 1878, and a declaration that the Assembly of 1890 expressly sanctioned what the Assembly of 1878 expressly declined to accept, viz., an understanding that these views of Dr. Dods, even in their present more offensive form (through the addition of the term " immoralities "), are henceforth " to be tolerated within the Church, and are not condemned by the Confession." The decision makes that " concession " to Dr. Dods, and to all of his way of thinking, which was expressly denied to him by the Assembly of 1878,—" a concession " for which, in his letters to the College Sub-Committee, he cannot sufficiently express his satisfaction, which he describes as " wise and great," and which he interprets as meaning that " our doctrine of Scripture may possibly need revisal." That is the " concession," forsooth, which is to mark a new era in the progress and prosperity of the Free Church. " Errors " in the original Scriptures, " immoralities " " commended, or even commanded " in the Old Testament,—these are to be the watchwords of the third Reformation, which our higher critics tell us is about to dawn on a country benighted by its " Bibliolatry " ! ! !

And our higher critics are infatuated enough to suppose that the people of Scotland are prepared to respond to such watchwords, and to rejoice in the prospect of thus getting rid, in this enlightened age, of an infallible Book, even as before they got rid of an infallible Pope ! ! ! They flatter themselves that by thus getting rid of the infallible Book, they will better succeed in bringing men to the infallible Christ, and Dr. Dods complains that many "sceptics have been made by claiming for Scripture an adhesion and a faith which belong to Christ alone." I know of no one who claims for Scripture such an " adhesion " and such a " faith." At all events, one of my chief aims in my ministry has been to warn men, that, like the Jews, they may be great Bible readers, and may have great regard for the letter of Scripture, and yet never come for life to Him of whom the Scriptures testify. But because men are saved by coming to Him and believing on Him, are they at liberty after they have come to Him to reject His testimony regarding that Book, through whose teaching they found their way to Him? Nay, verily. On the contrary, faith in Him, which brings about oneness with Him, also makes more precious than ever to the soul that Word of God, whose infallible truth and Divine authority were so emphatically endorsed by Him, and in which His voice continues to be heard.

This afternoon I stood by the bedside of a dying believer, and witnessed her calm trust, her holy joy, her heavenly peace as she quoted one text after another. Each text was to her as a light in the valley —the sure word of promise of a present precious Saviour. What an impertinence it would have been on my part if I had dared to offend this "little one" of Christ, by insinuating doubt into her confiding soul, by speaking of " mistakes," " inaccuracies," " discrepancies," " errors," " immoralities." In our evangelistic efforts also, we have surely difficulties enough without having them aggravated by currency being given under quasi-ecclesiastical sanction to forms of expression, which, as applied by the populace, will prove destructive of all faith in the Bible, in Christianity, in Christ.

I write strongly because I feel strongly, and because I am afraid that those who seem bent on having at all hazards ecclesiastical toleration for the view that there were "errors" in the original Scriptures, and that "immoralities" are "commended, or even commanded" in the Old Testament—and that too without any detailed specification of what is intended—have not yet realized the mischievous effects that are being wrought among the people by the down-grade movement now inaugurated.

I observe that though your letter refers to a public question, and to my action in public, you have marked it "private." I have no objection to our correspondence being made public, and as the College Sub-Committee declare that "a case has arisen not for disciplinary measures, but for grave, respectful, and considerate discussion," while the whole Church is interested in the question, I see no reason why, when for the third time, you, of your own accord, have written to me in regard to it, our friendly discussion should be "private." If your views are right, and mine are wrong, you ought to have the courage of your convictions, if now you have attained to settled convictions on the subject. I will respect your wishes as to the non-publication of your letter if you still so desire, but I hope that, in view of the state of the question and the public interests involved, you will not regard me as doing aught amiss if I treat this letter to you as *open*. Although I am far from being persuaded with Dr. Dods, that "nothing but good can result to our Church and to the Christian people of this country" from "grave, respectful, and considerate discussion"—although great evils are, I fear, likely to follow from the reiteration of words so offensive as "errors" and "immoralities" in connection with the Holy Scripture—I am prepared to face these risks, in the hope that some of the misconceptions that have gathered around the subject may be eventually removed, and that if we do not in the end see eye to eye, we may at least come to a better understanding as to the real question at issue. Meanwhile with kind regards, I am, yours very truly,

ROBERT HOWIE.

REV. DR. BLAIKIE.

Prestwick, *July 3rd*, 1890.

Dear Dr. Blaikie,

I have been so busy that I have been under the necessity of delaying my reply to yours of the 20th ultimo until I came here for my holidays.

I am unwilling to misapprehend your views, but regret that, notwithstanding the questions I put to you in my last on purpose to elicit from you a clear statement of your views, you have not yet given me any means of coming to a better understanding as to what they really are. Certainly you have not shown me wherein I have either misapprehended or mis-stated them when I last wrote you. On the contrary, the statements you now make, taken in connection with your previous utterances on the same subject only make plain that you hold that there are "discrepancies," not apparent but real "discrepancies," "inaccuracies," "errors" in the original Scriptures; that you hold that inspiration did not guard against these. In other words, I understand that your position is precisely the same as that of Dr. Dods, so far as the affirmation that there are "inaccuracies" or "errors" in the original Scriptures is concerned, although like him you doubtless would restrict these "inaccuracies" or "errors" to matters "unimportant or less important," and contend that they do not affect the infallibility of the Bible as a Rule of Faith and Life. This is perfectly consistent with your affirmation that "the inspiration of the Holy Spirit was always such as to secure that the great truths of Divine Revelation should be expressed in clear, suitable, and sufficient language, but not such that the direct authority of the Spirit should be claimed for every word employed."

Do you not see, that here you use a description of the effect of inspiration which might be applied to any sermon preached by a minister of Christ in the nineteenth century? He may express "the great truths of Divine Revelation" in "clear, suitable, and sufficient language."

Your failure to use the expression *truthful* or *accurate* as applied to the language of the Bible, and your repudiation of the direct authority of God for every word employed, make it impossible for you to base an argument even for a Biblical doctrine upon any word used in the Bible. You virtually condemn Christ and His Apostles for basing arguments upon words of Scripture (*e.g.* John x. 35, Heb. ii. 8, Gal. iii. 16, and Heb. xii. 27).

You say, " What concerns me is this: At a time when the Church seems to be slowly getting light as to God's method of giving forth and recording His revelation, you and others seem bent on driving us to a view (you don't like the word, theory) of inspiration which the Church has not yet formulated and which may henceforth be found to be wrong."

My view as to the *product* of inspiration (for as to its mode or "method" I do not profess to have got the "light" of which you speak) is, as I said in my last, that which is described by the College Sub-Committee as the "older view"—not caricatured—viz.: that "all the statements of the original Scriptures are true in the sense Divinely intended: that sense being also consistent with a fair use of words within the range of legitimate human speech."

I asked you whether you refused to endorse that as a statement of your personal belief, and as you give no answer to my question I presume you wish me to understand that you do not endorse it. That is apparent from the fact that you describe it as "an extreme view," to which "you desire not to be committed," and as one which "may henceforth be found to be wrong."

When you thus write, and when you further declare that it is a view "which the Church has not yet formulated," you surely have forgotten the language of the Confession of Faith? If there is one thing clearer than another in the Confession, it is that while the Confession gives no theory, and makes no statement as to the *mode* or method of inspiration, it makes statements as to the *product* of inspiration, which can have no other meaning, than that "all the statements of the original Scriptures are true in the sense Divinely intended: that sense being also consistent with a fair use of words within the range of legitimate human speech." What else can be the meaning of the Confessional statement:—" God (who is Truth itself), the Author thereof "—the Author, that is, of the whole Bible (the books of which are specified), not merely of some parts of it relating to things important, or to doctrine and duty? Manifestly the parenthetical words " who is Truth itself " are introduced by the authors of the Confession for the very purpose of excluding error from Holy Scriptures as originally given by its Divine Author through inspired men. Plainly, they would have regarded it as akin to blasphemy to affirm that the God of Truth—the God " who is Truth itself "—has been or can be the Author of " error." By calling its Author " Truth itself " the Confession stamps with the seal of infallibility whatever the Bible originally contained.

The result of this Divine Authorship is indicated with equal clearness by the assertion in the Confession of "the infallible truth and Divine authority thereof." That is again of the whole Bible—for there is no distinction drawn between some parts of the Bible to which these words apply, and others to which they do not apply. How you reconcile the affirmation that there was error in the original Scriptures with these statements of the Confession, I am at a loss to understand. In view of these statements of the Confession, I hold that I am fairly entitled to say that you, and those of your way of thinking, are the innovators in this matter, and that you " seem bent on driving us " to a view of inspiration utterly inconsistent with that which the Church has formulated in her Confession. Your conduct seems to me the more inexplicable, inasmuch as, with myself, you have subscribed the Confession. If you have discovered that the doctrine in regard to Holy Scripture there formulated is wrong or "may henceforth be found to be wrong," or if, with Dr. Dods, you wish the Church to "recognize that our doctrine of Scripture may possibly need revisal," you ought courageously to raise the question of the revision of the statements of the Confession on this point in the Confession of Faith Committee.

That certainly seems to me a far more straightforward course than to sign the Confession and yet to hold views which are inconsistent with its statements—for, as I have already said, when it speaks of Divine Authorship and of consequent "infallible truth and Divine authority," it draws no distinction such as you wish to draw between things important and things unimportant in the Bible, between some parts of the Bible which refer to doctrine and duty, and other parts which have not such an obvious reference.

You cannot deny that the interpretation I have given of the meaning of the Confession is that which has prevailed within the Church up till last Assembly. The Assembly of 1878, on the question being raised in the former case against Dr. Dods, affirmed that the doctrine of "the infallibility and Divine authority of Holy Scripture" is "contained in the Standards," and emphatically condemned the view that there were "errors in the Scriptures as originally given." Nay, more, in explicit terms it declared that it did not accept the understanding embodied in the letter of Dr. Dods to the Presbytery of Glasgow, viz., that the views expressed in his sermon and preface, then withdrawn, "are to be tolerated within the Church, and are not condemned by the Confession."

As the Assembly of 1890 has given an interpretation of the meaning of the Confession the very reverse of that given by the Assembly of 1878, it seems to be now absolutely necessary that this question be authoritatively decided, if the Church is henceforth to give forth a certain sound in regard to an article of faith so fundamental as the doctrine of Holy Scripture. If you and your friends mean to insist on having toleration permanently given within the Church to the view that there were "errors" in the Scriptures as originally given (not to speak meanwhile of the no less offensive term "immoralities"), I hope that you will not consider that we act unreasonably when we ask that you produce a complete list of the "errors" which you think you have discovered, and that you give us some more conclusive proof than has yet been offered that they were in the Scriptures as originally given. This is the more necessary as I find that scarcely any two persons are agreed as to what are the so-called "errors," even in our present Scriptures, while I have never yet found any one who has offered any proof of a convincing kind that any error whatever was in the Scriptures as originally given. Perhaps I should qualify this statement to the extent of saying that from a pamphlet of Count Agénor de Gasparin I have ascertained that M. Sherer, of Geneva, who, forty years ago, propagated the same views as those now advocated by Dr. Dods, did in point of fact, when challenged to give a specimen of an "error" in the original Scriptures, cite the case of the Centurion to which Dr. Dods has recently given so much prominence. The result was that the Count devotes a whole chapter of the aforesaid pamphlet in giving a reply so conclusive and crushing, that in view of it I am surprised that Dr. Dods, if he ever saw the pamphlet of Gasparin, has ventured to cite the same incident as a case of "error." But while Dr. Dods and M. Sherer are thus agreed in citing the same incident as a specimen of error in the Gospel narratives, I have been not a little amused to find that scarcely a single one of the most enthusiastic of the supporters of Dr. Dods has ventured to regard it in the same light, while your cases of so-called "discrepancy" have similarly provoked a smile even among these supporters of Dr. Dods.

As these facts make it plain that different minds will come to different conclusions as to what are to be regarded as "errors" even in our present Bible, we are surely entitled to have a list submitted to us of the so-called errors, and to have some proof furnished that they were all in the original Scriptures, so that we may know to what extent the Bible requires to be expurgated. You surely do not mean that every minister of the Church is to be at liberty to reject just as much as he pleases of the Church's supreme Standard on the ground that it is erroneous, and that, too, after he has solemnly declared before ordination or induction that he believes " the Scriptures of the Old and New Testament to be "—not to contain, but to be—" the Word of God."

If that is not your meaning, will you kindly say where the line is to be drawn? Will you explain how each minister and how each reader of the Bible is to be able to distinguish between what is true and what is erroneous in the Bible, between what is important and what is unimportant. Besides, if the sacred writers erred on other matters, what guarantee can I have that they did not also err in respect to doctrine and duty? If there were in the Scriptures as originally given any real errors, however trifling, then the men who wrote the Bible were not infallibly guided by the Spirit of God, at least, in some matters; and if not in some, what proof have I that they were infallibly guided in any? On what principle can you affirm that their infallibility extends to doctrine and duty if it does not extend to other things? Don't you feel the force of the questions which Dr. Adam is constrained to put when he admits that this view for which you contend involves " tremendous risks "? " Here," said he, " was a principle, and where were they to stop in its application? Here was a chink, would it not open, would it not widen until the whole flood came rushing in ? "

If you admit error in what you call unimportant matters, how can you object to the criticism of Row, who holds your view as to inspiration, when, in his Bampton Lectures, he treats as nontrustworthy the Biblical account of the creation, the antiquity of man, and the deluge? Once admit this principle, and every man will, according to his own theological standpoint, draw for himself the dividing line between the true and the false in the Bible. He will be able by this principle not only to get rid of such facts as he does not care to believe, but of such doctrines and duties as do not commend themselves to his acceptance.

To your credit, be it said, you have taken a greater interest than any other minister of our Church in the churches of the Continent, and I have no doubt that you are familiar with the outcome of the views of M. Sherer in Geneva. Here is what Count Gasparin says on that point :—" The head becomes giddy in following his career.

The doctrinal assertions even of his letters were alarming; but what progress has he made since? From one article to another, from one number to another of the *Strasburg Review*, the advance is frightful. We have noted, day after day, these melancholy and inevitable steps; and yet when we found them traced over in a few eloquent pages by M. Bonnet, we have been startled, as by a new and unexpected discovery. An inexorable logic has unfolded in swift succession the consequences of the principle laid down. Once delivered from the external authority of the Scriptures,—once sent back to the internal authority of his own religious conscience, and to a historical knowledge of the facts of Christianity,—M. Sherer has rejected both that which offends him and that which he does not comprehend! All this was very natural. Once led to reject in this manner a part of the Scripture, he has been compelled to ask himself why Jesus Christ had admitted it in its entireness. Thence followed the conclusion (which we scarcely dare to express), that Jesus Christ had accommodated Himself to existing notions, or that Jesus Christ was mistaken!—a blasphemous conclusion,—an emphatic condemnation of the principle from which it has been legitimately inferred."

I hope you will not deem it presumptuous in me to ask you to ponder these words of Count Gasparin and the evidence they supply as to the kind of developments we may expect in Scotland, if there is to be unlimited permission to affirm that there were errors in the original Scriptures. Surely the facts stated by the Count (and they are confirmed by what has taken place in other continental countries) may well lead evangelical men, like yourself, to pause in your attempt to commit the Free Church to this down-grade movement. At all events they show conclusively how grossly you are deceiving yourself when you claim that in adopting such views you are getting "light as to God's method of giving forth and recording His revelation." Although that is doubtless far from your intention, you are simply taking the first step towards popularizing in Scotland, if that be possible, the Rationalism of the continent, which is beginning already to be discarded in the lands in which it had its origin.

When I made it plain in my last letter that I attach chief importance to the testimony of Scripture writers regarding their own writings, and to the testimony of Christ and His apostles in regard to Holy Scripture, I am surprised that in your reply you take no notice of what I say on these points. In the light of the conclusion to which M. Sherer was logically led in regard to our Saviour, I will be glad to know how, in view of the manner in which He uniformly deals with Scripture, you hope to be able, with the view you hold as to there being errors in the original Scriptures, to avoid coming to the same conclusion as M. Sherer in regard to Him. If you are fairly to induct your view from "the statements and facts" of Scripture, I humbly submit that you are not at liberty to leave out of account the *main facts*. To use the words of Dr. Watts on this subject, in an able article which appears in the *Belfast Witness* of the 27th ultimo, and which I commend to you for perusal, your "methodology is based upon one of the most palpable of all logical fallacies—a narrow induction—a fallacy, which in this case, sets up a human inference against a positive Divine affirmation."

After what I said in my last letter in explanation of the difficulties you raised about the two versions of the Decalogue and the speech of Stephen, I do not feel that I ought to return at length to these cases of alleged "discrepancy," notwithstanding the prominence you again give to them. You appear to me to stumble because you have no correct apprehension of the function of inspiration in connection with reported speeches. On this point let me quote the words of Dr. Fairbairn:—
"Written as it (*e.g.* the Bible) is with much variety of form, containing a revelation from God made in diverse manners, as well as at sundry times—and assuming often the form of narrative and dialogue—it cannot intend, when asserting its immediate connection with the Spirit of God, that every portion, viewed singly and apart, is clothed with Divine authority, and expresses the mind of Heaven. For that, it would require to have been cast throughout into the form of simple enunciations or direct precepts; and all conversational freedom of discourse, and expressions of thought and feeling, adverse to the truth, must have been withheld. In speaking, therefore, of the inspiration of Scripture, respect must be had to the distinctive characteristics of its several parts. And where the sentiment uttered, or the circumstances recorded, cannot, from its obvious connection or import, be ascribed to God, the inspiration of the writer is to be viewed as appearing simply in the faithfulness of the record, or the adaptation of the matter contained in it to its place in the sacred volume. Were it but a human idea, or a thought even from the bottomless pit, yet the right setting of the idea, or the just treatment of the thought, may as truly require the guidance of the unerring Spirit, as a report of a message from the upper Sanctuary."

In the light of what is thus said by Dr. Fairbairn I again ask, Are you prepared to affirm that we have not a truthful report in Deuteronomy of what was said by Moses on the plains of Moab, or in Acts of what was said by Stephen? If we have a truthful report then my view of the effect of inspiration in the case of reported speeches is verified in both these cases.

You cite, as against my view, the words of Deut. v. 22, "These words the Lord spake unto all your Assembly ... with a great voice, and He added no more, and He wrote them on two tables of stone and delivered them unto me." Did it never occur to you, that in this verse Moses evidently used the term "words" in the sense in which it was often used as denoting the Ten Commandments delivered from Sinai? While, as I said in my last, he quotes these Commandments freely in a hortative discourse (and for proof that he did so I refer you again to Dr. Fairbairn's article on the Decalogue), he declares that these ten great "Words" or Commandments were spoken unto all the Assembly, written on two tables of stone, and delivered to himself, and that there were no other "Words" or Commandments added to them. Really before you try to convict Moses of error you must be sure that you understand the sense intended by him, when he uses the term "Words." But that apart, even if you could prove that Moses blundered in his speech by professing to give a verbatim account of what was on the two tables while he failed to do so, my view of inspiration is verified if we have in Deuteronomy a truthful account of what he actually did say on the plains of Moab.

And the same thing holds good in regard to the report of the speech of Stephen. If it is truthful my view of inspiration is verified, even although Stephen made a mistake about the sepulchre.

You seem to think that you can evade the force of what I said in my last letter on this point by citing certain expressions used about Stephen, as that he was "a man full of faith and of the Holy Ghost," also "a man full of faith and power," while reference is made to "the wisdom and the spirit by which he spake." From these expressions you seem to infer that he spake by inspiration of the Holy Ghost, and you argue that this is a case of an inspired man falling into "error." Are you warranted in drawing this inference? Is not every Christian commanded to be filled with the Spirit? May he not be so filled? May he not be "full of faith and power?" May we not refer to "the wisdom and the spirit" by which he speaks, without implying that his utterances are inspired in the sense in which the writings of the Old and New Testaments are inspired?

But even, if, as you suppose, Stephen spake by inspiration in the proper sense of the word, I hold that in view (1) of possible explanations which have been given which reconcile the account of Genesis and Acts, and (2) the fact attested by various readings that errors have through transcription found their way into our present Bible, you are not entitled to affirm that this is a case of proved "error" in the original Scriptures.

At best yours is a gratuitous assumption, which you cannot establish, for you cannot produce the original text to show that there was "error" there, even if you are perfectly sure that there is "error" in the speech of Stephen as reported in our present Bible. You know that sufficient time elapsed between the date of Stephen's speech and that of the oldest extant MSS. for the corruption of the text at this point.

For aught you know an older MSS. may yet be discovered, which would cover with confusion those who so confidently assert that there was "error" in the original text. Nay more, for aught you know, such additional facts in the lives, or in connection with the burial of the patriarchs may yet be brought to light, as may make it manifest that after all there is no real discrepancy between the speech of Stephen even as reported in our present Bible and its narrative in Genesis. What if it should turn out that Abraham did in point of fact buy a piece of ground near Shechem, although we have no account in Genesis of such a transaction, and that the buying of it led to a further purchase by Jacob? What if it should turn out that, as suggested by some of the best expositors, the word Abraham is an interpolation by a transcriber? What if the embalmed body of Jacob, after being buried in Machpelah as we read in Genesis, was afterwards removed (as the bodies of some of the heroes of more modern times have been removed from one place of sepulture to another) to Shechem to be laid alongside of the bodies of his own family—perhaps at that very spot, not far from Jacob's well, which was pointed out to us as Joseph's tomb? Other possible explanations I might have given on the supposition that Stephen spoke by inspiration in the strict sense of the word. I am not called upon to say what may turn out to be the correct explanation. In all such cases of acknowledged difficulty we need to know more about all the circumstances before we are in a position to determine which of several suggested explanations is the correct one, or whether there may not be some other possible explanation of a satisfactory kind in reserve.

As Westcott says, "Even in these passages which present the greatest difficulties, there are traces of unrecorded facts which, if known fully, would probably explain the whole." The difficulties of Scripture are vanishing quantities. Many of them that once appeared the most formidable have not only been solved, but have supplied new proof of the absolute truthfulness of Scripture in all its details. In presence of these facts, I think we may reasonably ask that you and others will have a little more patience in the interpretation of Scripture before asking the Church to give permanent toleration to a view of the Scriptures as originally given, which we conscientiously regard as not only fraught with the most mischievous consequences, but as directly contrary to the statements of Scripture writers regarding their own writings, and as subversive of the testimony of Christ and His Apostles regarding Scripture.

I shall be glad to have further explanation of your views if you still think that I have to any extent misapprehended them. I will also be glad to have your permission to publish your letters to me, reserving as I do my right to publish my letters to you.

With kindest regards and genuine respect, I am, yours very truly,

ROBERT HOWIE.

APPENDIX II.

WHY speak of "possible developments," involving a "denial of the Supernatural," as pertaining only to the future? Has not a "Christian evolutionist" (just returned from a trip to foreign parts) opened the Glasgow F.C. College by an address in which, from beginning to end, he advocates, so I understand him, the most undisguised *Naturalism*, in its baldest possible form? In keeping with his creed, he gives a striking illustration of the rapidity with which "development" may take place in the beliefs even of men who have signed the Confession of Faith. As he is one of the special admirers of Dr. Dods, and is generally credited with having not a little to do with moulding his views, this clear indication of the kind of "development" of the "new critical views" to be expected is very significant.

I wonder what the Convener of the Foreign Mission Committee, who was present on the occasion, thought of the proposal to speak of "the Christian evolution of the world, instead of, or as at least, a change from, the evangelization of the world;" to substitute the view of the evolutionist, viz., that "the world was sunken and must be raised," for the old fashioned Biblical view—that announced by Jesus Christ as explaining His mission and atoning death, viz., that "the world was lost and must be saved"; to send out to the heathen, men of "culture," of the "highest originality and power," who were in doubt as to whether "the cut of their theology quite qualified them to be successors of Carey and Williams," were "too honest to go, on what might seem to them false pretences, to a work which, though they were not specially enthusiastic for it, they were yet entirely willing to face if duty called"—to face it, however, on the understanding, that they go forth feeling it to be their "duty to find out what God had sown there already," and "instead of uprooting their Maker's work, and clearing the field of all the plants that found no place in their 'small European herbarium,' should rather water the growths already there" (in other words, should water Hinduism, Mahomedanism, Buddhism, etc.), "and continue the work where the Spirit of God was already moving."

If I may judge from the sermon lately preached in my church, on the occasion of the ordination of a foreign missionary, and especially from the report made by him and Mr. Daly in regard to our Indian missions, Dr. Lindsay cannot have much sympathy with the kind of proposal made by his colleague. Evidently he thinks that in the Indian field we have already quite enough of the "culture" element in our Foreign Mission operations, and that the "new departure" should be rather in the way of giving greater prominence to that "popular evangelism," which Professor Drummond regards as out of place, and requiring to be superseded by Naturalism. I wonder whether Dr. Adam (who, in his Assembly speech, said, "Here was a chink, would it not open, would it not widen until the whole flood came rushing in?") will now come to the conclusion that we have already got enough of the "flood," that more vigorous action than has yet been taken is needed to close up the "chink," especially when, on the authority of Professor Drummond, we are assured that our "halls were never richer" "than at this moment" in the kind of men he describes.

Very likely that very fact may be urged by the leaders as a reason why they should take no action whatever, even as Dr. Blaikie pleads, that it would be "Quixotic" "to attempt discipline against half the Church." If half the Church endorses the advanced views just promulgated by Professor Drummond, or if the Church is prepared to allow them to be taught to her future ministers, the fact should be made apparent, so that some of us may seek (even though our doing so may be the occasion of "noise, discontent, and strife,") to ascertain what the people of the Free Church think of the ecclesiastical toleration of such views.

APPENDIX III.

As the Inscription upon the Cross is the favourite specimen of so-called "errors" given by those who defend the views of Dr. Dods; and as currency has been given to it in Alford's Commentary, I append a reply made to his remarks on this subject in the "Journal of Sacred Literature."

"THE INSCRIPTION UPON THE CROSS."

"ONE word more as regards this inscription! Much has been *written* and spoken upon it, and one of the great critical scholars of the day (the Dean of Canterbury) makes the following observations, in his note on Matt. xxvii. 37 :—

'On the difference in the four Gospels, as to the *words of the inscription itself*, it is hardly worth while to comment, except to remark, that the advocates for the verbal and literal exactness of each Gospel may here find an *undoubted* example of the absurdity of their view, which may serve to guide them in less plain and obvious cases. *A title was written, containing certain words;* not *four titles, all different,* but *one;* differing probably from all these four, but certainly from three of them.'

May I venture to express an opinion, that these observations are somewhat *unadvised, contemptuous,* and *contradictory.*

1. *Unadvised,* inasmuch as Dean Alford seems to dismiss the subject at once with a remark which implies that there *are differences* in the manner of giving the inscription which are *irreconcilable.* Is this so? Are there differences which *are irreconcilable!*

2. *Somewhat contemptuous,* inasmuch as he evidently views all who hold the doctrine of *verbal inspiration* (if he means this, by '*verbal and literal exactness*') as guilty of consummate weakness and folly; whilst *we* who hold that doctrine feel that we are able to *defend* and *support* it by solid argument.

3. A *little contradictory,* inasmuch as he first of all states, 'a title was written,' '*not four* titles, but ONE;' and then adds, 'differing probably from all these four.' But '*one title*', and yet, after all 'FOUR' titles!

In noticing this little contradiction in his mode of expressing himself, I do not wish to be thought captious, but as the *satisfactory proof* of there being no *irreconcilable* difference between the four Evangelists as regards the inscription upon the Cross turns upon this point, viz., that there really was but *one title*, I am tempted just to notice it. That the Evangelists all differ, the one from the other, in their mode of giving the inscription upon the cross, is quite clear. Are then their differences *reconcilable?* Most assuredly they are.

I. John gives Pilate's 'title,' Ἔγραψε δὲ καὶ τίτλον ὁ Πιλᾶτος. Two other of the Evangelists give 'the ACCUSATION' against Jesus. *Matthew*,—Ἐπέθηκαν ἐπάνω τῆς κεφαλῆς αὐτοῦ τὴν αἰτίαν αὐτοῦ γεγραμμένην. *Mark*,—Ἦν ἡ ἐπιγραφὴ τῆς αἰτίας αὐτοῦ ἐπιγεγραμμένη. *Luke* simply gives the word ἐπιγραφὴ.

But what was the ἐπιγραφὴ? It is most reasonable to answer τῆς αἰτίας! Surely it is allowable to supply the ellipsis from *Mark*, whose words have been quoted.

II. What then was the TITLE?—Ἰησοῦς ὁ Ναζαραῖος ὁ βασιλεὺς τῶν Ἰουδαίων. What was the ACCUSATION?—Ὁ βασιλεὺς τῶν Ἰουδαίων. See Luke xxiii. 2; Mark xv. 18; John xviii. 33, 37; xix. 12, 14, 15. Thus *Matthew*,—οὗτός ἐστιν Ἰησοῦς ὁ βασιλεὺς τῶν Ἰουδαίων. *Mark*, —ὁ βασιλεὺς τῶν Ἰουδαίων. *Luke*,—οὗτός ἐστιν ὁ βασιλεὺς τῶν Ἰουδαίων.

There is no inconsistency, no want of agreement, no irreconcilable difference here. Each evangelist does what he *professes* to do. *John* professes to give the 'TITLE,' and he gives it! *Matthew, Mark*, and *Luke* do *not* profess to give Pilate's *title*, but the 'ACCUSATION' against Jesus, and they each of them give it. If *Matthew*, Mark, and Luke, or either of them, had used the word 'title' (in other words, had professed to give *Pilate's title*) there would have been a discrepancy between all, or either of *them*, and *St. John*, which it would perhaps have been difficult if not impossible to have harmonized. But each professes to give the '*accusation*,' and the '*accusation*' ONLY; and as long as they each give the '*accusation*,' (it matters not, whether it be simply given, as by St. Mark, ὁ βασιλεὺς τῶν Ἰουδαίων, or with an additional remark, as by St. Matthew, 'οὗτός ἐστιν Ἰησοῦς,' etc., etc., etc.; and by St. Luke, 'οὗτός ἐστιν,' etc., etc., etc.,) they each do what they *profess* to do; there is *perfect consistency* in their statements, and no semblance of *irreconcilable differences* between them. W. R. C. R.

Dowdeswell Rectory, Gloucestershire, April 23, 1864."

APPENDIX IV.

Dr. Blaikie, referring to the explanation of Turretine, says that "If Pascal in his 'Provincial Letters' had come across it, he would have had something racy to say of it!" If Pascal had dealt with this question, his "racy" things would not have been said in condemnation of the conduct of those who, in accordance with their professed creed, and their solemn ordination vows, do their best to repel the charges made against the Bible by "rationalistic interpreters"; to vindicate the infallibility of Scripture in all its statements; and to uphold the testimony of Him who said, "And the Scripture cannot be broken."

His scorn, his ridicule, his invective would rather have been reserved for the conduct of one who, before ordination and induction, publicly declared that he believed "the Scriptures of the Old and New Testament to be the Word of God," and publicly subscribed the Confession of Faith; who, so recently as May last, threw "a sop that missed Cerberus" (see *British Weekly* of June 6, 1890) by voting for a motion, which declares that the Church "views the use of the term 'mistakes and immoralities' to describe recognized difficulties in the Scriptures as utterly unwarranted, and fitted to give grave offence"; but who, for years, personally held and *privately* advocated the very views in the *apparent* condemnation of which he thus *publicly* joined (and that, too, although they were emphatically condemned by the Assembly of 1878), and only ventured to avow them *publicly* after he believed that he might do so with ecclesiastical impunity.

Of all the statements made by Dr. Blaikie, not the least astounding are those in which he seeks, on the one hand, to make it appear that the Assembly of 1878 "decided no principle," and on the other, to "deprive of all validity the argument founded on the article on Holy Scripture in the Confession of Faith." The opening part of the deliverance of 1878 was as follows:—"The General Assembly, considering that they are not in circumstances to enter with advantage on a discussion of the topics which this case appears to involve, and that no substantial interest appears to be imperilled by accepting the decision of the Synod, dismiss the protest and appeal, and declare the sentence of the Synod to be final." If words have any meaning, these imply that in declaring the decision of the Synod to be "final" the Assembly regarded itself as "accepting" that decision. And what was the decision of the Synod? It was as follows:—

"The Synod sustain the Complaint in so far as it takes exception to the Report approved of by the Presbytery as not being a full representation of the dangerous character of the views set forth in the Sermon and Preface reported on, especially in not with sufficient emphasis condemning the view that there are errors in the Scriptures as originally given; and the Synod, moreover, take this opportunity of affirming the doctrine which was endangered by said Sermon, and which is contained in the Standards of the Church, namely, the infallibility and divine authority of Holy Scripture; and, further, having learned from the bar, that the Sermon is now withdrawn, the Synod are of opinion that the case should here take end."

Not only did the Assembly declare that decision to be "final." It went further. After discussion, Dr. Rainy, who proposed the motion, which became the finding of the Assembly, was compelled to add to his original proposal the words:—"The Assembly do not accept the understanding expressed in Dr. Dods' statement engrossed in the Minute of Presbytery of Glasgow of 5th December, 1877." The "understanding" referred to was that the views embodied in the Sermon and Preface then withdrawn "are to be tolerated within the Church, and are not condemned by the Confession." The Assembly thus declared both what it did accept, and what it did not accept. It accepted the decision of the Synod and declared it to be "final." It did not accept the "understanding" of Dr. Dods. And yet in face of all this, Dr. Blaikie contends that the Assembly "decided no principle," and that the doctrinal views of the Synod are not "morally binding on the Church." His contention is based mainly on the fact that neither the Presbytery of Glasgow nor Dr. Dods appeared at the bar as appealing against the decision of the Synod. If that view is to prevail, parties interested in any case can henceforth, by falling from their appeals, prevent any finding of the Assembly from becoming "morally binding." A more complete travesty of both the law and the practice in civil and ecclesiastical courts it is scarcely possible to conceive.

There is a recognized order in Presbyterian Church courts for preventing any decision of an inferior court from becoming "morally binding" on an individual, viz., by the prosecution of an appeal to a final issue. If the appeal is dismissed, he who thus prosecutes it has at least freed himself of personal responsibility for the finding of the Supreme Court. He is substantially in the same position as those members of the Supreme Court who may dissent from its finding. Referring, in last Assembly, to the decision of the Assembly of 1878, Dr. Adam said that it "was not entitled to a great deal of respect," and that "if that Assembly had adopted the decision of the Glasgow Presbytery, and not the decision of the Glasgow Synod, he thought they would have been on safer ground." In these words Dr. Adam admitted that the Assembly did "adopt" the decision of the Glasgow Synod, and if he believed that they ought to have adopted the decision of the Glasgow Presbytery, it was his duty to have advised the Presbytery, after they had appealed, to appear at the bar of the Assembly in support of their appeal. But the Presbytery, on his motion, fell from their appeal. In these circumstances, it is somewhat strange that Dr. Adam should speak of that decision as "not entitled to a great deal of respect." It is no less strange that he should be supported in that contention even by Dr. Rainy, who moved the finding of the Assembly. When our leaders thus treat decisions, which they have themselves moved, or in which they have acquiesced, they can have no well founded ground of complaint against our present action. Many of us formally dissented against the finding of last Assembly. Others were, by the forms of the House, prevented from dissenting against a finding of which they personally disapproved, on the ground that they had previously voted for it (although it was notorious that they had done so, simply because in the final division they had no alternative, but either to do so, or to allow a still worse motion to become the finding of the Assembly). A still larger number were not members of the Assembly. In view of the practical reversal by last Assembly of the finding of the Assembly of 1878, and that, too, on the motion of those who acquiesced therein, we are surely justified in seeking to obtain an "equally authoritative declaration" from a future Assembly, such as will rectify the wrong done by last Assembly.

Referring to the Confession of Faith, Dr. Blaikie quotes a statement made by Mr. Ross Taylor, on the authority of Dr. Mitchell, viz., that "the Westminster divines were at special pains to leave open all reasonable questions as to the mode and degree of inspiration which could be consistently left open by those who accepted the Scripture as the infallible rule of truth and duty." Thereafter Dr. Blaikie says:—"This, I think, goes a long way to deprive of all validity the argument founded on the article on Holy Scripture in the Confession of Faith."

Whether Mr. Taylor correctly represents Dr. Mitchell, and whether Dr. Mitchell correctly represents the Westminster divines, I am not in a position to say, until I have time to consult the "original sources." But even on the supposition that what Mr. Taylor says on the authority of Dr. Mitchell, is true, I fail to see how it "deprives of all validity" the argument of our "Statement" in regard to the Confession. We did not need Mr. Taylor to tell us that the Confession lays down no theory as to "the mode and degree of inspiration." That is what I have again and again affirmed.

But while the Confession gives no theory as to the *mode* of inspiration, its statements as to the *product* of inspiration are quite definite. As we declare in the "Statement," the Confession identifies the Scriptures of the Old and New Testament (the Books of which are specified in detail), with the "Word of God written." "It makes no distinction between parts of the Bible relating to doctrine and duty, and other parts not so related." It speaks of "God, (who is Truth itself) the Author thereof," and of "the infallible truth and Divine authority thereof," *i.e.*, in each case of the whole Bible. Dr. Blaikie says, "that the phrases do not occur in it which the 'Statement' uses to denote its position, and that it is only by putting an interpretation which is not conceded by others on the phrase, 'God, the Author of the Scriptures,' that any claim to confessional authority can be advanced for the view of the 'Statement.'" I challenge Dr. Blaikie to cite a single phrase which the "Statement" represents to be in the Confession which cannot be found there. It is very amusing that in the very act of bringing such a charge of misquotation against us, Dr. Blaikie attaches marks of quotation to the phrase, "God, the Author of the Scriptures," although such a phrase is not found either in the Confession or in our "Statement." The words of the Confession which correspond to it are found in the fourth section of Chap. I., which the Assembly deliverance ignores, but which we correctly quote as follows: "The authority of the Holy Scripture, for which it ought to be believed and obeyed, dependeth not upon the testimony of any man or church, but wholly upon God (who is truth itself), the Author thereof; and therefore it is to be received, because it is the Word of God."

We say that this is " the part of the Confession which bears most directly on the question at issue. It was evidently introduced by the compilers of the Confession to assert the claim of Scripture to be received as objective truth. Manifestly the parenthetical words 'who is truth itself' were introduced for the purpose of emphasizing the fact of the absolute truth of the whole Bible. By calling the Author 'truth itself,' the Confession stamps with the seal of infallibility whatever the Bible originally contained." If these words of the Confession, and the words "the infallible truth and Divine authority thereof" which are found in the fifth section, do not exclude the view advocated by Drs. Dods and Blaikie, viz., that there were "errors" in the Scriptures as originally given, it will, I venture to say, be difficult to find words that will accomplish that object.

APPENDIX V.

IMPROVING THE BIBLE!

A PARABLE FOR TO-DAY.

A SOMEWHAT humorous, though not unreal, representation of the effect likely to be produced by the wild assertions so frequent from the lips of the newest school of Biblical critics appears in the columns of the *Boston Watchman*. A worthy deacon, accustomed from his youth to rely implicitly on the absolute trustworthiness of every verse within the boards of the Bible, heard with astonishment the new pastor declare that the opening chapters of Genesis were mythical, not literal; and were only intended to express with emphasis the unity of God, so as to counteract the polytheism both current and common at the time when they were written.

On his return from church he asked his wife to bring him the scissors.

"What do you intend to do with them?" she answered.

"Did you not hear our new pastor tell us these earlier chapters of Genesis are myths? and, as I don't want any myths in my Bible, I am going to cut them out."

She pleaded with him not to spoil the old Bible they had so often read together and had learned to love so well; but he was deaf to all her expostulations, stoutly maintaining that, instead of spoiling he would improve it by removing what was untrue; and the offending chapters were accordingly excised.

Not many Sabbaths had passed when the deacon again called for the scissors. On this occasion the whole Pentateuch was doomed to disappear. In answer to the remonstrances of his wife, he said quietly, yet firmly,

"Our pastor, who is a learned man himself, declares that 'the best scholarship' is thoroughly convinced that Moses did not write these books; that they are merely a collection of pamphlets from various sources, some Assyrian, some Egyptian; and, moreover, their contents prove that, in part at least, they were written centuries after the death of Moses."

So the whole Mosaic literature was ruthlessly cut out.

Not long after the scissors were again in requisition. This time they were employed in removing the latter half of Isaiah, who was thus literally "sawn asunder" for the first, if not the second, time, the reason given being these words of the pastor: "While he would not say that he fully believed they were not written by Isaiah, the son of Amoz, yet the higher criticism of the schools had declared that some unknown author, or some unknown Isaiah, had added the last twenty-five or thirty chapters."

In due time, an exposition of "scholarly doubts" concerning the genuineness of the Fourth Gospel succeeded in securing its severance from the sacred volume. With little difficulty the deacon was persuaded to part with the Books of Ruth, Esther, Ecclesiastes, and the Song of Solomon; while the story of Jonah was so shattered with shafts of ridicule that it was speedily cut out with a sigh of positive relief.

Sunday after Sunday the scholarly pastor pointed out an interpolation here and an interpolation there, all of which were forthwith extinguished, as the deacon "didn't want any interlopers in his Bible."

For two whole years these amendments continued, and then the deacon asked his wife to accompany him on a visit to his spiritual teacher. Being asked if he intended taking his Bible with him, he answered gravely, "Certainly I do, for I am anxious he should see how the 'higher criticism' and the 'best scholarship' have improved it."

When they called and were seated, the peculiar looking book the deacon had brought with him arrested the pastor's attention.

"What have you there, deacon," he asked.

"My Bible," was the reply.

"It is a queer-looking Bible; what have you been doing to it?"

"Well, now, pastor, I'll tell you. Every time you doubted any passage of Scripture, or said it was an interpolation, I have cut it out. All the books of doubtful authenticity are gone. The stories borrowed from the heathen nations, the myths, everything that you implied was questionable, I have removed according to your teaching. But thank God, my dear pastor, the covers of the good old Book are still left. All the rest is about gone, and I want to thank you so much for leaving me the covers."

The grim humour of this parable, freely translated from the American original, lies on the surface. Beneath, it is neither lacking in point nor in purpose. With a rare recklessness, and under pretence of superfine scholarship, certain pulpits are labouring week after week to rob the people of their Bible. If many men were smart enough to follow the example of the deacon in the story, some preachers would learn to think twice before insinuating doubts and gendering unbelief so freely as they now do. For it is precisely by these wanton attacks on Holy Scripture, made by the men who have sworn to defend it, the uncertainty as to the veracity of the Bible, so prevalent to-day, has been produced, and is still steadily maintained.—*Word and Work*.

POSTSCRIPT TO SECOND EDITION.

I. Since the First Edition was issued, I have looked into the Theological Lectures of Dr. Cunningham for confirmation of the allegation made by Dr. Blaikie that he starts with a "presumption" in favour of "plenary verbal inspiration," &c. I find that although Dr. Cunningham states one consideration which "affords, at least, as strong a presumption in favour of the doctrine of verbal inspiration as its alleged non-necessity does against it"—(in other words, repels one "presumption" by another "at least as strong")—he is so far from basing any argument on "presumption" that, in the very passage from which the quotation cited by Dr. Blaikie (p. 5) is taken, he says:—"We are not entitled to pronounce dogmatically beforehand either that it [verbal inspiration] was or was not necessary for effecting the ends which the Bible was intended to serve." Nor is that all. On the following page, which surely cannot have escaped the eye of Dr. Blaikie, Dr. Cunningham says:—"But, after all, the question under consideration is one of fact, and must be decided by the appropriate evidence applicable to it as such; and the only sources from which we can get any authentic information upon the point are either the statements of Scripture, if there are such, bearing directly upon the topic, or the Scripture viewed as a whole, and by its general character and complexion as well as by its specific features, indicating something concerning its origin and composition. The first of these sources is much the most satisfactory and authoritative, because as the divine commission of the authors of the books of Scripture, and even the truth and accuracy of all its statements, are admitted by those with whom we are at present arguing, its authority must be conclusive upon the question, if it has indeed afforded any materials for deciding it; while mere inferences from the general characteristics of Scripture must be liable to great uncertainty" (p. 349).

In view of the position now taken up by our opponents (viz., that there were "errors" in the Scriptures as originally given), it is noteworthy and suggestive that Dr. Cunningham thus affirms that, by those with whom *he* was arguing, "the divine commission of the authors of the books of Scripture, and even the truth and accuracy of all its statements" were admitted.

Dr. Cunningham's views ought not to be matter of dispute. Here are his own words:—"Contradictions and inconsistencies have indeed been alleged to exist in the Sacred Scriptures, and these have been often adduced and urged, not only by infidels, but even by men who, while professing to believe in the truth of the Christian revelation, have refused to admit the divine origin and authority of the books which compose the Bible" (p. 287).

II. I have received from Professor Drummond a letter (marked "private") of date November 28, in which, referring to Appendix II., he says:—"I repudiate it utterly as representing anything I said or could say. From beginning to end it is a travesty. You have put words into my mouth which I never spoke, and left impressions which I abhor as much as you do." At the same time he complains that I had made an attack "upon a brother presbyter without first communicating with him," and adds: "I must trust to your sense of honour to make the amends that are necessary, both in the next edition of your pamphlet and in the newspapers." As he thus condemns my public action, and calls upon me to take further public action, why does he trammel me by marking his letters "private"? The reason he assigns is that thus he "will least expose" me "to shame." Having done nothing of which I feel ashamed, I for my part am quite willing that our correspondence should be published.

While expressing my satisfaction with the above emphatic repudiation, in my reply I called the attention of Professor Drummond to the fact that every statement I attributed to him was quoted from the report of his inaugural address, as given in the *Glasgow Herald* of November 5.

His utterances were public. The report of the *Herald* was very widely circulated, and has in many quarters produced a most unfavourable impression; and it appears to me that if that impression is false, either because of something being attributed to the speaker which he did not say, or because of the incomplete nature of the report, it is clearly *his* duty, not *mine*, to correct it. In view, both of the particular statements quoted and the whole trend and tenor of the address as given in the *Herald*, I do not feel called upon to modify the comments contained in Appendix II. (excepting always the reference to the late Dr. Adam), comments founded on the report in question. Were Professor Drummond to publish his address, adding, if necessary, such notes or comments as will make it impossible for his meaning to be misunderstood, the whole matter would be set right. As to the Professor's complaint, surely a distinction must be drawn between beliefs privately held and quasi-privately promulgated, and an Address delivered at the opening of a College Session—an Address, the *Herald* report of which was widely circulated, for good or evil, before being noticed by me, and which has not yet been publicly corrected by the speaker. It is high time that this whimpering on the part of certain Professors about private dealing before attention is publicly called to their published utterances should come to an end.

III.—I have just seen Dr. Blaikie's "Second Edition with Postscript."

The Postscript is most valuable. I did not begin the controversy with him. As already shown, he had privately made known to me that he held the very views expressed in his published Letter, but he objected to my bringing them before the public. He cannot but have known that I was a party to the "Statement" on which he publicly animadverts, and which he describes as "a most uncharitable document." He may find fault with the manner in which I have met his animadversions, but it must not be forgotten that I was either defending a position which Dr. Blaikie assailed, or else, under a misapprehension as to his real views, I must have been fighting a man of straw. In other words, the position taken up in the "Statement" and in my "Reply" must be accepted or rejected by Dr. Blaikie. In view of the complaint he makes in his Postscript about misrepresentation of his "object" and of his "theological position," I am still at a loss to know exactly where he wishes to stand. The question at issue is simply this:—"Are all statements of the original Scriptures true in the sense divinely intended: that sense being also consistent with a fair use of words within the range of legitimate human speech?" On that question I argue for the affirmative, and (as I understood) Dr. Blaikie for the negative. But it now turns out, notwithstanding all he has written about discrepancies and errors, he complains that I affirm that his "object is to show that there are 'errors in the Bible.'" If I have been mistaken on this point, I shall only be too glad to find myself in the wrong, and to have him henceforth standing by my side in contending that there were no errors in the original Scriptures.

It is unnecessary to follow Dr. Blaikie into the details of his Postscript. I leave the readers of his "Letter" and of my "Reply" to judge whether there was not good ground for all my allegations.

The "Statement" he criticized was the result of much thought and of much prayer. It appealed to the ministers and office-bearers of the Church on questions of vital importance. Dr. Blaikie's Letter was obviously intended either to discredit that document or to minimize its importance.

My Reply was not "official," as he insinuates. But after his previous correspondence with myself, I could not sit silent and allow to pass unnoticed the strictures contained in a "Letter" written by one deservedly held in high esteem by the whole Church, and one whose orthodoxy has been unquestioned. An attack made by him on the "Statement" could not fail to be regarded as of more importance than if made by one with a doubtful reputation. While I express myself strongly on some points, I have been anxious not to misrepresent Dr. Blaikie on any particular. I have not classed him with "Rationalists." The single expression he cites (from page 9) is found in a quotation from

Krummacher, and refers to the Germany of his day. While quoting Krummacher's words as evidence of the logical and practical outcome of the views defended, as I understood, by Dr. Blaikie, I am so far from classing him with Rationalists that (p. 51) I speak of his " evangelical standpoint," while (pages 11 and 12) I quote with approbation from his excellent article on "The Old Pulpit and the New." If anywhere I may seem to have classed him with a school, it was only because of his advocacy of the views of that school—an advocacy all the more effective, because of his pronounced Evangelicalism.

It is with no little satisfaction that I learn from the Postscript that instead of vindicating Dr. Dods, Dr. Blaikie has adopted an opposite course. Referring to the expression I used (viz., "eagerness to vindicate Dr. Dods to the utmost"), he says: "No one knows better than Dr. Dods how ridiculously incorrect that statement is." I further observe, that in the New Edition Dr. Blaikie has omitted Appendix IV. of his First Edition, at the close of which the following words occur:—" Having recently had occasion to read with care some of Dr. Dods's more extensive expository writings I bear my cordial testimony to the great good I have got from them and their quickening and elevating tendency." What does this omission mean? Does it imply that the more recent utterances of Dr. Dods, and especially his lecture on "The Seat of Authority in Religion" (reported in the *Christian World* of Nov. 20) have so startled Dr. Blaikie, that he now thinks it prudent to withdraw the certificate just cited?

Having affirmed (at p. 19) that "to sift Scripture, and accept or reject statements because we like or dislike them, is contrary to the first principles of Protestantism," Dr. Blaikie can scarcely fail to be staggered by that latest utterance of Dr. Dods, in which, as I understand him, the individual conscience is declared to be the supreme arbiter as to what parts of the Bible are to be accepted or rejected—the doctrine taught in his Sermon and Preface published in 1877 but subsequently withdrawn.

The omitted Appendix has also an important bearing on the question of Dr. Blaikie's "inconsistency" in publicly joining in the apparent condemnation of views which he privately advocated, and which, as he now tells us, he has "openly avowed" to his students "for a dozen or fifteen years." That Appendix admitted that the votes Dr. Blaikie had "given in the Dods' case" required "some explanation," especially when he there frankly declared:—"allowing for exaggeration, I am not far off from Dr. Dods's view." The omission of that Appendix, taken in connection with the complaint he makes against me in the third paragraph of his Postscript, is surely significant.

The words on which he remarks in paragraph four of his Postscript were quotations, and it is hard that after I had done my best to show that the "weakness" of his production was "due, not to want of ability" on his part, but to "the essential weakness of the cause he seeks to defend," he should "reward" me by describing my endeavours as "skits and flings." Dr. Blaikie gives new proof of his skill as a controversialist in that, while he makes so much of these "minor" matters in my "Reply," he does not once attempt to grapple with its arguments.

After my criticism of them, the omission from the New Edition of the following words (page 9 of the First Edition) is very noteworthy:—"Don't let us go into hysterics over this. There is some tendency of this kind even in the deliverance of the Assembly." No less noticeable are the words now added (page 11) in the New Edition, viz., "I grant, too, that some of your opponents have been fearfully indiscreet." I hail both the omission and the addition as evidence that it is beginning to dawn on Dr. Blaikie that the compilers of the "Statement" are not so far wrong after all. Before attaching too much importance, however, to the added words, we would need to know precisely what Dr. Blaikie means when he says, "fearfully indiscreet." Does he mean that by his blunt "forms of expression" and his "intemperate" utterances, in season and out of season, Dr. Dods has needlessly awakened anxiety and called attention to the dangerous character of his views, and that he would have acted more discreetly in following his own example? If that is his meaning, I have no hesitation in saying that, much as I differ from Dr. Dods and deprecate many of his public utterances, I have far more respect for his conduct when, having the courage of his convictions, he manfully tells his Church what he holds and means to teach to her students (braving all the consequences of such an avowal), than for the conduct of one who is "not very far off from Dr. Dods's view"; who, as Professor, has for twelve or fifteen years taught his views to the future ministers of the Church, though the views of Dr. Dods were condemned by the Assembly of 1878; who while doing so not only failed to tell the Church that he was thus engaged, but even as late as May last joined in the apparent condemnation of the views of Dr. Dods; and who only openly avowed his own views before the Church at large after he had apparently persuaded himself that because of the decision of last Assembly he might do so "with ecclesiastical impunity!"

www.ingramcontent.com/pod-product-compliance
Lightning Source LLC
Chambersburg PA
CBHW020331090426
42735CB00009B/1496